"Every once in a while, one encounters a book and exclaims: 'Of course, what a needed book. Why hasn't someone done this before?' *There's No Place like Home* is that kind of book. What a wonderful gift to women who feel called to leave the marketplace and return home! If you're that women, you're going to love this book. It's practical and it's biblical. Also, if you're that woman, you are going to rise up and call Mary Larmoyeux and Ethan Pope blessed."

Steve Brown
Professor, Reformed Theological Seminary, Orlando, Florida
Bible teacher, *Key Life* radio ministry

"Moms, no one can do the job of raising your child as well as you! If you have been yearning–even just a little–to become a full-time mother, you need to read this book. It's filled with practical answers, strategies, and encouragement–plus lots of real life stories and spiritual helps. It will inspire you and give you hope!"

Barbara Curtis
Author, *Small Beginnings* and *Ready, Set, Read!*
Montessori teacher, frequent MOPS speaker, mother of 11

"If you are a Mom who wants the opportunity to be at home full time with your children, this book is an answer to your prayers. *There's No Place like Home* is a common sense manual to help working moms–who desire to be home–get there!"

Josh McDowell
Director of Josh McDowell Ministry

"Finally, a common sense, step-by-step plan that will enable moms to go home. I wish every young married couple would read this book before they have children! This book will help couples work through the thorny decision making process and show them how they can win where it matters most–at home!"

Dennis Rainey
Executive Director, *FamilyLife*

# There's No Place Like
# HOME

## STEPS TO BECOMING A STAY-AT-HOME MOM

# There's No Place Like

# HOME

STEPS TO BECOMING A STAY-AT-HOME MOM

Mary Larmoyeux and Ethan Pope

BROADMAN
& HOLMAN
PUBLISHERS

Nashville, Tennessee

0–8054–2376–1

Published by Broadman & Holman Publishers, Nashville, Tennessee

Dewey Decimal Classification: 306
Subject Heading: MOTHERS

Unless otherwise noted, Scripture quotations are from the Holy Bible, New International Version, © copyright 1973, 1978, 1984. Other versions are noted by acronym as follows: KJV, King James Version. NASB, the New American Standard Bible, © the Lockman Foundation, 1960, 1962, 1963, 1968, 1971, 1972, 1973, 1975, 1977; used by permission. NKJV, New King James Version, copyright © 1979, 1980, 1982, Thomas Nelson, Inc., Publishers. NLT, the Holy Bible, New Living Translation, copyright © 1996. Used by permission of Tyndale House Publishers, Inc., Wheaton, Illinois 60189. All rights reserved.

Library of Congress Cataloging-in-Publication Data

Larmoyeux, Mary, 1951–
      There's no place like home : steps to becoming a stay-at-home mom / Mary Larmoyeux and Ethan Pope.
            p. cm.
ISBN 0–8054–2376–1 (pb.)
1. Mothers–United States–Case studies. 2. Housewives–United States–Case studies. 3. Motherhood–United States–Case studies. 4. Parenting–United States–Case studies. 5. Motherhood–Religious aspects–Christianity. 6. Parenting–Religious aspects–Christianity. I. Pope, Ethan. II. Title.
HQ759 .L372 2001
306.874'3–dc21

2001025526

1 2 3 4 5 6 7 8 9 10   05 04 03 02 01

This book is dedicated with love to my husband, Jim.

—Mary Larmoyeux

This book is dedicated to all the working moms who have a longing in their hearts to be at home with their children full-time. It is my prayer that God will use this book to help you accomplish your goal. Even if it only helps one mom to move from the workplace to the home place, it will be worth all the effort!

—Ethan Pope

# Contents

# Foreword

## By Beverley LaHaye

"I want to be home!" It's a story that I hear across the country from countless other moms. They are in the workforce, but their hearts are at home with their children. My heart breaks for these women, for I know many of them feel trapped due to personal debt, the need for health insurance, or just to make ends meet. And our national culture and government do not make it easy for a family to choose to have mom stay at home instead of going back to work.

But moms, let me assure you that it is well worth whatever sacrifice it requires of you and your family for you to be at home. The decision you make now will affect your entire family, your children's futures, and yes, even the future of our country. I have worked for more than twenty years to protect the family in America, and I can tell you that your decision to guide your children through their growing years at home will impact this country tremendously!

In the late 1960s and throughout the 1970s, feminism gained unprecedented popularity throughout America. Women were told they should be "equal" to men. The work of a mother at home with her children was demoralized, leading millions of women to believe that they needed to have a career to be worth something. So women joined the workforce en masse, all believing the feminists' mantra that they "could have it all." The Equal Rights Amendment was debated in congress and state legislatures across the nation. Feminists, politicians, and political commentators discussed how to start a national child-care program.

By the mid-1980s, however, we began to see the cumulative effects in our culture. A new phrase was added to our national lexicon:

*latchkey kids.* Millions of children went home from school each day to face an empty house. Millions more children spent their days in a day-care setting. And we saw other changes. Divorce rates skyrocketed, as did juvenile crime rates. Educational test scores went down, and drug use among preteens and teens went up dramatically. No one was at home to nurture the family, and it began to break down.

Now we live in a country where the majority of children under one year of age have mothers in the workforce. And the fastest growing segment of working mothers is comprised of mothers with children under six years of age. Since 1960, this group of mothers has tripled their workforce participation. What a national tragedy!

Many women now realize, however, that by trying to "have it all," they are in danger of losing it all. The stress involved where both parents are trying to raise a family and maintain a career can be overwhelming. Many of you have come to the place where you realize that your career is just not worth the toll it takes on you and your family. And your heart may long to be home, but you just don't know how to get there. Sadly, many of you must work due to divorce, the death of a husband, or other unique financial constraints. But so many more of you can be at home with your children. You just need the tools to help get you there.

Mary Larmoyeux and Ethan Pope approach this subject beautifully. They give a thoughtful and practical guide to prepare you emotionally, spiritually, and financially to go back home. Written from their hearts and their wealth of experience, Mary and Ethan provide just the tools many moms need. For it is one thing to want to stay at home, but it is another to make it work in reality.

In particular, I appreciate the importance they have placed on your spiritual preparation. Moms, this is a crucial point. For it is God who will mold your heart, and your husband's, to prepare you for this big change. And he will enable you to make the changes, even when you cannot see how it can be done. I encourage you to pray through this decision, alone and with your husband or a close friend. Prepare to grow spiritually!

Once you have made the decision to leave work and stay at home, let me encourage you to persevere. You will almost certainly face doubts and uncertainties, financial and emotional. But take heart! There are countless other women facing the same pressures and doubts. Be active in searching for friends, play groups, or support groups with women who are also at home with their children. Having a network of other women around you will be essential to your goal of staying at home.

Finally, let me commend you for your decision! Once home with your children, you will certainly see the difference it makes in your children's lives and the life of your family. But it will also make a marked difference in the life of our nation. Mom, you will be able to guide your children morally, physically, spiritually, and emotionally. You will be able to take action in their lives—and in the community affecting their lives—in ways you never could while working. Your work at home will affect how your children develop and the world in which they live.

Moms, my heart and prayers go out for you! Your work in raising your children matters. The spiritual and moral guidance you give them now will affect them for a lifetime. And no one else can do it the way you can. Then family by family, we just may see a generation of young people grow to lead this nation and restore our moral integrity.

# Acknowledgments

## MARY

Ethan and I both thank God for allowing *There's No Place like Home* to become a reality. We pray that the Lord will use it to help many, many moms!

Ethan, it's been great working with you! I am very grateful for your professional expertise in the financial arena and for your heart to help mothers. Len Goss, thanks for encouraging Ethan and me and for guiding this book into reality. We appreciate you and the team at Broadman & Holman Publishers.

To my husband, Jim; sons, Chris and John; our small group at The Summit Church; and many friends, thanks for your ongoing prayers and encouragement!

To the moms who shared your stories, saying "thank you" seems inadequate. May God bless you in a special way for your willingness to help others.

Betty Dillon, Sarah Farley, Jim and Chris Larmoyeux, I cannot begin to tell you how much I appreciated your taking time to read the unedited manuscript to this book. Your feedback was so helpful, and your suggestions have surely made this a better book.

To you, the reader, thanks for carving out time from your undoubtedly busy life to read this book. May God grant you the desires of your heart.

## ETHAN

Thanks to all the moms who shared their stories with me during the writing of this book and to the hundreds of moms who responded to my surveys. I am indeed a better person because of my interaction with you.

It has been such a joy to coauthor this book with Mary Larmoyeux and to work with Leonard Goss and Broadman & Holman Publishers.

Most of all, thanks to my wife, Janet, who not only believes the principles being taught in this book but has also put them into practice every day since our first child was born in 1984.

# Introduction

## MARY

If you are a working mom, do you long to be home with those you love? Or perhaps you don't yet have children, but you yearn someday to be a stay-at-home mom. As a working mom myself, I know exactly how you feel. Ethan and I pray that God will use this book to grant you the desires of your heart.

Last year my husband, Jim, taught a class at our church based on Ethan Pope's book *How to Be a Smart Money Manager.* This book is packed with practical advice, making even difficult financial topics seem simple.

I had finished writing the book *My Heart's at Home: Encouragement for Working Moms,* when Jim taught the class on financial principles. I couldn't help but think about working moms as we went through our sessions. I had met Ethan once at FamilyLife in Little Rock, Arkansas (where I work), and I knew that he was a solid Christian. He and his wife had been on staff with Campus Crusade for Christ prior to beginning their own ministry, Foundations for Living.

I thought, *Lord, I have a heart for working moms. I know their plight and believe that most of them would really like to be home if they could only figure out how to do it. And I know that Ethan has the know-how to help these moms.*

And so I asked Ethan if he would be interested in coauthoring a book that would help mothers stay at home with their children. He and Janet prayed about this and decided that they would indeed like to help moms. I believe that God has divinely orchestrated our paths to intertwine so that we could write this book and help you get home!

1

My son, John, is now at Marine boot camp. Although he is near the ocean in San Diego, he has not been allowed to leave the training base. He wrote that he knows he is near the ocean because he can hear and see the seagulls. Imagine smelling the fresh salt water, hearing the shrieks of the gulls, watching them swoop down–knowing they are diving for fish. But you just can't see the vast, mighty ocean or feel its cool waters! How frustrating!

I think this is a picture of the working mom whose heart is at home. She knows what home is like. She can smell the fresh scent of her baby. She has heard the chatter of her two-year-old. She can imagine the first steps, games in the backyard, and afternoons snuggled up in an oversized chair, reading to her little ones. But she can't seem to figure out how to get home. Frustrating? You and I know it is! Probably not only for her, but also for her husband.

We are told in Psalm 37:4, "Delight yourself in the LORD and he will give you the desires of your heart." Mom, I believe if you truly delight yourself in the Lord, he will show you how you can stay home with your children if that is truly a desire of your heart!

As we journey together through the pages of *There's No Place like Home,* I will share stories and situations of women just like you. And Ethan will give you a clear road map that can get you where you want to be–at home! After all, there is absolutely, positively no place like it!

ETHAN

If the culture in which we live ever needed a book, this one would definitely rank in the top ten. As I looked over my list of goals for writing projects (books, articles, etc.), not one project was on moms leaving the office and staying at home. But when the opportunity was presented for me to coauthor a book with Mary on this topic, I knew in my heart it was the right thing to do. It was time to change my priorities. I talked the project over with my wife, and she wholeheartedly endorsed and encouraged my involvement in writing this book.

I am committed to helping any mom who desires to stay home to do just that! This book is not about condemning moms who are presently working outside the home. It is about helping moms fulfill their God-given role at home by providing them with biblical and practical information about how they can move from the marketplace to the home place. Or, for some moms who are faced with tremendous financial pressure to go out and find a job, how they can still remain at home.

Many of the points in this book might appear to be written to "convince" a mom to leave the marketplace, but they all must be taken in the context in which they were written: "To encourage, motivate, and help moms who desire to move from the marketplace to the home place." Don't pass judgment on this book unless you have read it from cover to cover. In fact, if you have no desire to move from the marketplace to the home place, let me encourage you not to read this book.

This book was written specifically for the mom who is crying out to God and longing within her heart to leave the workforce (or not enter it) and to stay home because she believes God has called her there. She will do whatever it takes to accomplish her goal! Yes, for most families it will be a financial sacrifice for mom to stay at home. But in the opinion of this author and his wife, it's worth it!

Just look at the statistics that are shaping our families and our nation today:

- Of the 103 million women sixteen years or older in the U.S., 61 million were labor-force participants during 1995.[1]
- Women accounted for 59 percent of labor-force growth between 1985 and 1995.[2]
- Women earn only 75 cents for every dollar earned by men.[3]
- In 1996, 70.2 percent of working moms had children at home that were eighteen or younger.[4]

The working mom has become the cultural norm, even the Christian norm. But does it have to be? Can we do anything to turn the cultural trend? Who will have the courage to be different? Where can a working mom go to find answers? Can a family actually live on just one income? How does a family prepare spiritually, emotionally, and financially for mom to move from the workplace to the home place?

These are the questions Mary and I will be attempting to answer in our book. We want to offer solutions for your family, and we will be praying that God will mightily use this book in your life. Nothing would please us more than for you to be at home with your children! After all, there is no place like home! And we want *you* to be there!

CHAPTER 1

# Our Journey Begins

### MARY

Delight yourself in the LORD, and he will give you
the desires of your heart.

–Psalm 37:4

Have you ever gotten lost while traveling? Perhaps you found yourself in the middle of a busy intersection, and you just weren't sure which way to go. You may have hoped that the direction you took really didn't matter–that somehow you would end up where you wanted to go. But whether you realized it, the decision at that crowded intersection probably determined your destination. At such a time a good map would have seemed priceless.

Since you are reading this book, I imagine that your destination is home. Perhaps you want to plan today how you can stay at home when you have children. Or maybe you are seeking directions to get you on that path. Proverbs 20:18 reminds us to "make plans by seeking advice." Our prayer is that God will use this book to turn your desire to stay at home into a reality. We pray that this book will be the "good map" you need.

The Pew Research Center (www.people-press.org/momrpt.htm) stated: "Contemporary motherhood is a balancing act for many women. Fully half of American women with children under eighteen now work full time, and the biggest challenge they face, in their own words, is dealing with time pressures attendant to being a mother as well as a worker and a wife. . . . Women, whether or not they work,

5

believe the more traditional setting, in which the father works full time and the mother stays home is best for raising children."

The Family Research Council reported that "about one-third of all married mothers in this country are employed full time year-round. Another third are non-employed women who chose to stay home with their children. And the final third are mothers employed part-time or part year. Contrary to media reports, many of the mothers employed identify more with the mothers-at-home than career women employed full-time. Many of them work at home or organize their employment schedules around their husband's or children's."[1]

As Ethan and I begin writing this book, please understand that we are not passing judgment on anyone who feels that God has led her to work outside the home, to be a stay-at-home mom, or to work in the home. Larry Burkett wrote in his book *Women Leaving the Workplace,* "The truth is that working a full-time job should not be classified as a sin; nor should stay-at-home moms be viewed as drop-outs." The purpose of *There's No Place like Home* is to show moms how they can be at home with their kids. Nothing would thrill Ethan and me more than for God to use this book to allow you to spend more time nurturing your children and cherishing the short time that you actually have with them.

If I could turn back the pages of time, I would certainly have been a stay-at-home mom. My husband, Jim, and I thought that we were working towards this but did not have a definite blueprint to make this desire a reality.

I have a card that says, "A goal without a deadline is only a dream." The older I get the more I realize this truth. Our prayer is that God will use this book to help you develop a clear, workable plan—with deadlines—so that you can stay at home with your children. We believe there is no more noble profession than to be a wife and mom, a nurturer and molder of tomorrow's leaders. And since you are reading this book, you probably feel the same way.

Jim and I have been married for over twenty-five years. As a young girl, all I ever wanted was to be a wife and mother. I wanted to stay home with my children but ended up being a working mom. Looking back, it's easy to see why my dream did not become a reality: the premature birth of our oldest child, Chris; my husband's choosing to become self-employed at the very time that I "quit" work to be with Chris; the expenses of sending children to Christian schools—I could go on and on.

Ethan's and Janet's story is different from Jim's and mine, and yours is different from ours. Actually, all of our stories are unique! Ethan's mom did not work outside the home during the early years of his life. He writes:

> I will admit, it was great growing up in a home where mom was always there! My dad was dying of cancer during the early years of my life, and my mom had to spend a lot of time with him in the hospital, but I knew that her heart was really at home—and that gave me a great sense of love and security as a young child.
>
> My dad died nine days before my eighth birthday. About a year later, my mom returned to the workplace as a schoolteacher in our hometown. She did not return to teaching math simply out of her love for teaching, but for financial reasons. She now had the total responsibility to provide for her family, which included herself and three children! Believe me, if anyone understands why some moms have to work, it's me. I am proud of my working mom, and I thank God for her! However, I am convinced to this day that if given the opportunity to have remained at home, she would not have entered the workplace but remained at home full-time to nurture and raise our family.
>
> I joined the full-time staff of Campus Crusade for Christ in 1978 and worked with Campus Crusade for Christ for ten years. I spent my first two years on campus staff at Auburn University and the remaining eight years working with the Josh McDowell ministry in Dallas, Texas. I will never forget in January 1978, when Dennis Rainey (executive director of

FamilyLife) came and spoke at our new staff training. He explained God's blueprint for the family as I had never heard before! It was so simple and so clear! He explained the role of the husband and the role of the wife and God's design for the family. This was the first biblical teaching I had ever received on how the Christian family should look and operate.

It was during this same staff training that I met Janet, my wife to be. After a great friendship, which eventually led to a dating relationship and engagement, we were married in Orlando, Florida, on May 29, 1982. It was our personal conviction that when we had children, Janet would not work outside the home. It was also the policy of Campus Crusade for Christ. On April 21, 1984, God blessed us with our first child, Natalie Joy. At that time Janet stopped working full-time and became a full-time mom and wife.

God blessed us with our second child, Austin Alexander, on September 10, 1986. We remained full-time with Campus Crusade for Christ until 1988. At that time we decided to begin our own ministry called Foundations for Living. Even after leaving the staff of Campus Crusade, we carried with us the conviction that Janet was to remain at home and my responsibility (with God's help) was to provide 100 percent of the financial needs for our family.

Did we have some hard years financially? *Yes.* Did we ever seriously consider Janet's working outside the home? *No, not really.* Even sixteen years after the birth of our first child, we are still convinced it was the right decision for Janet not to work outside the home but to be a full-time mom and wife.

You might be asking, "How did you and Janet do it?" To be honest, it was not easy living on a modest ministry salary compared to what other couples were earning in the workplace. However, as I look back at how we did it, several things come to mind.

- It was a goal and biblical conviction that we had for our family. Janet working outside the home was never really an option for us.

- We had to do without some of the things that many other families with both parents working were able to have–nicer clothes, newer cars, eating out more often. Yet during these years we seldom felt that we were without anything we really needed.

- We had to maximize the limited resources God had entrusted to us, and the only way we could accomplish that was to plan and operate on a budget.

- Even though we had limited means, we were always faithful in financially supporting the kingdom of God. God was always faithful to meet our needs every month, and we remained faithful to give.

- We never forgot the God factor. We took God at his Word and placed our trust completely in him to meet the physical, spiritual, and emotional needs in our family.

Now that our children are teenagers, Janet is taking a more active role within our public ministry. She now is involved in traveling and speaking at women's conferences. Since we are in a different season of child rearing, we feel completely comfortable with Janet beginning to work outside the home.

Well, mom, the Popes began their marriage far differently from the way Jim and I did. They had definite God-given goals, and they had a plan (even a budget!) to reach them. Jim and I had talked about how we wanted our lives to be when we had children. I wanted to be a stay-at-home mom, and Jim totally supported that. But we did not have a plan (and did not have a budget!) to make this a reality.

Through the pages of this book, I will share a working mom's heart and hopes with you. Ethan will help you develop a workable financial plan to get home.

The birth of this book began when Jim and I went through a study of Ethan's book *How to Be a Smart Money Manager.* I realized where we went wrong financially when I read what Janet said about goals: "You must have a purpose for your life, a goal that is so big it makes everything else that you want seem small. You must have a goal that is worth any sacrifice, any hardship, or any suffering. You must have a goal that consumes your thoughts and motivates your soul. You must have a purpose so that when you look back at the end of your life, you will have no regrets. That goal will help you focus on the important things in life!"[2]

Jim and my story is very different from Ethan's and Janet's. I realize today that staying home with the children was not really a genuine goal. Yes, it was a genuine desire. But, somehow, a "new" car (even if it was secondhand), a bigger house–for the growing family, Christian education for the kids pushed this desire to the background. Had my staying home been a goal bigger than life, then the education, car, and house would have had to fit around it. As a young couple, Jim and I simply did not understand the financial ramifications of early choices in our marriage. And believe me, we were not alone in this.

Lynn Brenner wrote, "Most Americans have no formal education in basic economics or in personal finance, which is its practical application. Making financial decisions is as essential a skill for an adult as driving a car–but, unlike Driver's Ed, economics isn't a required high school course in most states." She went on to say that "on average, adults got a grade of 57 percent on the basics of economics. Among high school students, the average grade was 48 percent."[3]

It is amazing to realize that most American adults do not have a good grasp of economics. A lot of us do not really understand what it will take financially for us to stay home with our kids. Jim and I have learned a lot from our mistakes, lessons we hope will help you.

This book gives you biblical financial advice, woven in the lives of real women just like you. God promises us in James 1:5, "If any of you lacks wisdom, he should ask God, who gives generously to all without finding fault, and it will be given to him." Psalm 37:4–5 tells us, "Delight yourself in the LORD and he will give you the desires of your heart. Commit your way to the LORD."

A friend of mine sent me a note saying that his wife, Angela, "would like to be able to stay home with Jessica and any future children we have. Maybe someday she can."

*Maybe someday*–his words echoed in my mind. I remembered a young mom who had similar thoughts long ago. And those somedays are now gone forever.

If you are an Angela–wanting to stay home with your children or future children–then this book is for you! I believe that God has orchestrated my path and Ethan's so that you can confidently take steps in a definite direction that will lead you where you want to go. Possibly you have already made some choices, and you find yourself traveling through an unexpected detour. Ethan's expertise and godly wisdom will help you get back on the right path toward home.

I remember a speaker who once put some large rocks into a clear, glass jar. After doing this, he poured a container of sand into this same jar–everything fit perfectly. However, when he poured the sand into the jar and then tried to put in the large rocks, they just would not fit, no matter how hard he tried to force them into it.

He explained that the large rocks are like our priorities. When we plan our day around what really matters, everything falls into place. When we don't, then our main priorities will just not fit into our limited time.

That's how it is in life, Mom. Prayerfully decide today your major priorities–what is bigger than life for you and your family. Then be sure that your actions match your priorities, that they are first and do not get crowded out by the less important.

Ethan and his wife, Janet, once lived in a lovely neighborhood in Dallas, Texas, in a beautiful redbrick two-story home. It was a wonderful home, with a spacious yard and tall trees. But after living in this home for only three years, the Popes felt a call by God to launch a ministry called Foundations for Living. This became a burning desire, a goal so big that it made everything else seem small. They sold the home and purchased a more economical one.

If Ethan and I were to ask you and your spouse, "What are your goals in life?" What would you say? Do the following exercise, adapted from *How to Be a Smart Money Manager* to understand one another's priorities.[4] After completing the exercise independently, compare your list with your spouse's.

## HUSBAND'S GOAL-SETTING EXERCISE

Establish your priorities (from 1 to 18) on the following list, making your highest priority number 1. You cannot use a number more than once. You must rank all 18.

_____ Establish a business.

_____ Pay for college expenses for our children.

_____ Have more children.

_____ Pay off credit card debt.

_____ Give more to church.

_____ Ensure that mom can stay home with the kids (or future kids).

_____ Tithe.

_____ Buy a home.

_____ Pay off the home mortgage.

_____ Set up a retirement fund.

_____ Leave our children an inheritance.

_____ Make a major purchase of (furniture, carpeting, etc.).

_____ Buy a car.

_____ Provide a Christian education for our children.

_____ Operate our family on a budget.

_____ Acquire more education for myself.

_____ Help relatives who are ill or in failing health.

_____ Other: _____

## WIFE'S GOAL-SETTING EXERCISE

Establish your priorities (from 1 to 18) on the following list, making your highest priority number 1. You cannot use a number more than once. You must rank all 18.

_____ Establish a business.

_____ Pay for college expenses for our children.

_____ Have more children.

_____ Pay off credit card debt.

_____ Give more to church.

_____ Ensure that mom can stay home with the kids (or future kids).

_____ Tithe.

_____ Buy a home.

_____ Pay off the home mortgage.

_____ Set up a retirement fund.

_____ Leave our children an inheritance.

_____ Make a major purchase of (furniture, carpeting, etc.).

_____ Buy a car.

_____ Provide a Christian education for our children.

_____ Operate our family on a budget.

_____ Acquire more education for myself.

_____ Help relatives who are ill or in failing health.

_____ Other: _____

## COMPARISON OF HUSBAND'S AND WIFE'S GOALS

Jot your responses below in the appropriate spaces.

H    W

\_\_\_\_  \_\_\_\_  Establish a business.

\_\_\_\_  \_\_\_\_  Pay for college expenses for our children.

\_\_\_\_  \_\_\_\_  Have more children.

\_\_\_\_  \_\_\_\_  Pay off credit card debt.

\_\_\_\_  \_\_\_\_  Give more to church.

\_\_\_\_  \_\_\_\_  Ensure that mom can stay home with the kids (or future kids).

\_\_\_\_  \_\_\_\_  Tithe.

\_\_\_\_  \_\_\_\_  Buy a home.

\_\_\_\_  \_\_\_\_  Pay off the home mortgage.

\_\_\_\_  \_\_\_\_  Set up a retirement fund.

\_\_\_\_  \_\_\_\_  Leave our children an inheritance.

\_\_\_\_  \_\_\_\_  Make a major purchase of (furniture, carpeting, etc.).

\_\_\_\_  \_\_\_\_  Buy a car.

\_\_\_\_  \_\_\_\_  Provide a Christian education for our children.

\_\_\_\_  \_\_\_\_  Operate our family on a budget.

\_\_\_\_  \_\_\_\_  Acquire more education for myself.

\_\_\_\_  \_\_\_\_  Help relatives who are ill or in failing health.

\_\_\_\_  \_\_\_\_  Other: _____

Now discuss your individual goals and compare your answers. Do you have the same goals?

Now each—husband and wife—should write down what you learned from this exercise.

If mom's staying home with the kids is one of your top priorities, then read on. With God's help, this book will give you practical, biblical advice that can turn your dream of being a stay-at-home mom into a reality.

Scripture tells us in Psalm 27:14, "Wait for the LORD; be strong and take heart and wait for the LORD." And we are told in Isaiah 58:9,

"Then you will call, and the Lord will answer; you will cry for help, and he will say: Here am I." It is an awesome thought to consider that the God who created the universe loves you and me. And he wants to be actively involved in our lives and put our feet on level ground— if we will only let him!

Do you remember Dorothy saying in the *Wizard of Oz,* "There's no place like home!"? Mom, there is no place like home, and *you can* be there with your kids!

**Scriptures to Ponder**

"In his heart a man plans his course, but the LORD determines his steps" (Prov. 16:9).

"For which one of you, when he wants to build a tower, does not first sit down and calculate the cost to see if he has enough to complete it?" (Luke 14:28 NASB)

**Action Steps**

Write on a piece of paper where you are in your personal journey. Are you presently at home and desire to remain at home? Are you currently working but headed for home?

Assuming you have already made the decision to remain at home or to move from the marketplace to the home place, take a few minutes and write out your specific goal about remaining at home or getting home. Place it on a three-inch by five-inch card and put it on your bathroom mirror to remind you every day of your destination. Pray daily that God will give you his directions for your journey.

## CHAPTER 2
# Off to Work I Go

### MARY

Women around the world, especially mothers, are more likely than men
to say they feel stressed, a global survey of 30,000 people shows.

—Lynn Brenner

Stress hormone levels in working mothers rise each morning
and stay high until bedtime, putting them at higher risk than
other working women for health problems such as heart attack,
according to a study by Duke University Medical Center researchers.

🐾 If you are a mother who works outside the home, I'm sure you
have experienced the pressure of juggling home and work responsibilities—especially if your heart longs to be at home with those you
love. You know so well those signs of a stressful day—when you can't
remember the names of your own children or whether you
unplugged the curling iron. And when you put the newspaper in the
refrigerator, watch out!

Too often we moms act as though we are supermoms, and many
in society say that we can be everything to everyone. You and I both
know that supermom never existed and never will. But a lot of mothers are working today, and many are trying to do it all.

Exactly how many moms work, you ask? *The Statistical Handbook
on the American Family* stated, "In 1996, 53.6 percent of wives/moth-
ers whose husbands were present in the home and who had no children under the age of 18 were employed compared to 70 percent of
mothers with children in that age group. Mothers with young children had a rate of labor force participation a few percentage points
lower than mothers with older children."[1]

Ethan and I know that moms like you, whose hearts are at home, work for many reasons: to help pay for unexpected expenses, to get out of debt, to pay for medical expenses and Christian education. The reasons are as many and varied as there are different families. When I entered the workforce as a young mother, my husband and I did not consider the added pressure that outside work would bring into our home. (I also planned to work for only a year or two.) For all moms, especially those working outside the home, there are just not enough hours in the day. No wonder more and more mothers are wanting to exchange the workplace for the home place.

Paul Harvey wrote:

> Women fought long and hard for a place in the
> workplace. Next, they sought and won acceptance in the
> executive suite. However, gradually, their pay scale is moving
> up to match that of men. Now the prize they sought is
> diminished by the cost it cost. The Yankelovich survey each
> year has asked working women if they would quit their jobs.

> "If you didn't need the money, would you quit your job?"

> For the first 20 years of the survey, about 30 percent of
> working women said "yes."

> By 1989, the number grew to 38 percent.

> The most recent survey shows that 56 percent of working
> mothers would like to go home![2]

As you will read in chapter four, Ethan's Mom Survey revealed that 64 percent of working moms would like to be at home! The question I have for mothers like you and me is not, would you like to be home with the kids? It is, how in the world can you *be* at home with your kids? I believe that millions of moms like you are praying that God will somehow show them a way back home. As I tell you the stories of Tina, Becky, and Traci, you very likely could be reading pages from your own diary. (The names of Tina, Becky, and their family members have been changed.)

When Tina was only eleven years old, it seemed that life had dealt her family an unfair, untimely blow. How could God have allowed the death of her father, a pastor of a small congregation? As the oldest of six children, Tina sensed that her life would be different from most children. And it definitely was.

Her mother had never handled finances before her dad's death, and the young widow was overwhelmed by these responsibilities. Tina began working when she was fourteen years old and gave most of her earnings to her mom for the family. It is easy for Tina to look back today and understand why she grew into a young woman whose main goal in life was to be financially stable. You see, her mother never was. And Tina was *not* going to be like her mother.

Tina met her husband, Charlie, when she was in college studying accounting. They had mutually agreed that Tina would finish her degree after they married and that someday they would have children. Tina recalls, "We never talked about whether I would stay home when we had kids.

"In 1994, my husband, a builder, started his own business. Between college loans and start-up costs, debt mounted quickly. We had always thought that we would turn around and pay it right off. He worked very hard while I was going to school full-time. We both had car payments at that time."

After their daughter, Beth, was born, and Tina stayed home with her for five months while she finished her college degree. "Those were the most glorious months. That's when I decided that I didn't want a career and that I wanted to be a stay-at-home mom. But we had tons of debt—debt from college and my husband's business. I thought I would work for two years and we would get the debt paid off. I thought it would be easy to catch up once I started working again."

Tina still vividly recalls what she felt when she first left Beth at day care. "Fear, anxiety, guilt, terror—I couldn't wait to get back to her. I wanted to be the one who cared for her, and I did not want to leave her in someone else's care. I wanted to be the one who made sure she was OK."

Now four years have come and gone, and Tina is still working. There are some pretty lean months in the building business and many unexpected expenses. "We had to put tubes in Beth's ears; that was $2,100. The health insurance did not pick it up."

A turning point came in Tina's life when Beth was about two years old. After a stressful day at work, Tina asked Beth to let her peel her banana. But Beth demanded (as only a two-year-old can) to do it herself. Rather than pulling the banana skin off quickly, the little girl kept trying to open it in a sawing fashion. In desperation she handed her mom the banana that now seemed more like banana pudding in a peeling. Tina thought, *God, this is a picture of me. I am making mush out of my life by demanding to do things my own way.*

It was then that Tina decided to look for a more family-friendly job. Working fifty or more hours a week as a supervisor in a CPA firm was taking a toll on her family. "The stress was killing me." She discussed her feelings with Charlie, and "we took a huge leap of faith." Tina took a $10,000/year cut in pay so she could work in a Christian ministry *just* forty hours a week. "It was a huge relief to be able to focus on my family," she said.

Tina realized that "all of my life my security has been in being financially secure. . . . My security needs to be in the Lord, and now I am seeking him daily." Tina is praying that if it's the Lord's will for her, she can somehow be a stay-at-home mom. Charlie has decided to go to work for a company. "After he gets steady pay, then we can reevaluate what we could save in day care."

Tina's advice to moms who would like to stay at home with their children is: "Don't create any debt. . . . Someday you will hold a gift from God more precious than any material thing you think you need. Give your desires to the Lord, and he will give you the desires of your heart."

Tina would agree with Dr. Brenda Hunter who wrote, "Decades of child-development research show that what all young children need to grow up emotionally healthy is a warm, affectionate relationship with their mothers."[3]

Becky, a first-grade teacher, also recognizes the importance of those first few years for children. As a little girl, Becky's only dream was to be a stay-at-home mom when her children were young. When her children were school-age, she wanted to be a teacher–just like her own mother.

Becky said: "To me it was the perfect job for a parent. When we were off for holidays and the summer, mother was off. . . . I felt called to teach, but I wanted to be at home with my kids when they were young."

What twist of fate could have prevented this nurturing mom from staying home with her own daughter during the preschool years?

Two words sum up the beginning of this story, *infidelity* and *divorce*. Her husband was overseas in the service, and he was actually living with another woman. Their marriage was shattered and with it Becky's plans to be a stay-at-home mom with Elizabeth. Instead she would enter the world of working single parents.

Never in a million years would Becky have imagined herself as working throughout the entire years of Elizabeth's childhood. Being an educator, she knew the importance of the first few years of life, and she wanted to be there for her daughter.

"I had to watch how much time I spent with teaching," she recalls. "Elizabeth was so important, and I wanted to spend time with her. So I would spend time with her and then stay up real late, getting ready for class the next day."

As a single mom, Becky was offered what some would say was the opportunity of a lifetime–a complete scholarship for her doctorate. Because the offer would mean a move away from her supporting family, she declined the offer. Even today she says, "I do not regret not getting my doctorate. The kind of person Elizabeth is today is worth far more than money."

Life has had many peaks and valleys for Becky, who is beginning her twenty-seventh year of teaching. She continues to marvel at God's continued faithfulness throughout her life. Her advice for young women who would like to stay at home with their kids is,

"Make that decision up front and don't get in debt where you feel like you have to work."

Mom, whatever your situation is, God knows all about it. Find comfort in Romans 8:28, "And we know that in all things God works for the good of those who love him, who have been called according to his purpose." Give your desires to be at home with your kids to the Lord, and trust him to do a mighty work for your family as he did in Traci Massey's home.

When Traci was a little girl, she dreamed of growing up to be successful. She explained her meaning of success to me as "having a nice home, nice car, and nice clothes." After her parents' divorce when she was three, her mom went back to work to support the family. So it is easy to understand why Traci just assumed that she would always work outside the home. She and Bill never even discussed whether she would work when they had children of their own.

But after working for almost seven years, Traci traded in a sales career that she truly enjoyed for home. She recalls, "Every day I would cry and think, *Why is my baby at home and I am on the road?* I had been appointed to sales manager, and my territory was an hour and a half north of where we lived and three hours south from where we lived. It bothered me that I was so far away from my child if anything happened. I felt I needed to be there. And I was missing all of the fun things."

She went on to say, "We had gotten on Ethan Pope's budget (MAP, Money Allocation Plan), and that is what started us thinking maybe we could do this. I was making almost as much as my husband was. For me to quit would cut our income in half. It was such an emotional issue that the budget was freeing. When we got on it, we thought maybe we could make it on Bill's income."

Traci says that there have been lots of changes in the way she and Bill now live. They have cut out spending on "clothing, eating out, the vacation fund, and recreation." But, she says, it has definitely been worth it. "My stress level went from a ten to a two. I feel like I am a better person to be around. The family can enjoy me more. I am not so full of everything but my family. I can relax, which I could not do before." She continued, "I am very glad I did this. . . . I am being a better wife to Bill because I can devote more time with him because I spend time with Lowery during the day."

Traci admits that the change has not been easy. She said, "It is hard when you give up an income. It takes a lot of obedience, and we have not always obeyed. We have to pray daily." But she is amazed by how the Lord has provided financially for them since she decided to quit her full-time job. When Lowery goes to preschool two days a week (from 8 to 11:30 A.M.), Traci is able to do some outside sales, and the Lord has really blessed her efforts.

Traci believes that she has been a better wife to Bill and a better mom to their daughter, Lowery, since coming home. But, she says, her greatest benefit is:

> I realized that for the first time in my life I had truly
> started to rely totally on the Lord. I was saved at an early
> age and had trusted the Lord as my Savior, but I rarely let
> him be Lord of my life. God has used this desire of my heart
> [to be home] to teach me how to trust totally in him with
> every aspect of my life. It feels great to have the peace that
> passes understanding. I know that life won't always be easy,
> and giving up an extra income will be trying, but I also know
> that I am now more equipped to handle these stresses
> through the Lord. I now have a freedom from a bondage
> that has controlled my life for a very long time.

Her advice to young women who would like to stay at home with their children is: "After the Lord has called you to do this, do it right away because he will provide. But you must be sure he is the one calling you." She also recommends, "Whether or not you want to be a stay-at-home mom, do not accrue a lot of debt because you have to pay it back. If you do have children and want to come home, it [debt] will make it more difficult. I thought I would want to work, and I do like to work, but I love [being with] my children and family. . . . The Lord will provide in amazing ways."

God has given Traci the time she desired with her family, to be at home with those she loves. Our prayer is that he will somehow use this book to allow *you* to be home with those *you* love!

Dr. William Lane said, "When God gives us a gift, He wraps it up in a person." Mom, you are a gift of the Lord to your children. He wraps his loving arms around your children through your arms! And there is no place like home to share God's abundant love with the legacy that he has entrusted to you.

**Scripture to Ponder**

"Do not be anxious about anything, but in everything, by prayer and petition, with thanksgiving, present your requests to God. And the peace of God, which transcends all understanding, will guard your hearts and your minds in Christ Jesus" (Phil. 4:6–7).

**Action Step**

Spend time with your spouse writing down things which cause anxiety in your home. Pray together that the Lord will remove these things from your lives and that your home will be a model of Christ's love and peace.

CHAPTER 3

# Six Reasons Most Moms Work

ETHAN

*Most Americans work until about May 10, just to earn*
*enough to cover their federal, state, and local taxes.*

If you have ever bought a home, you probably heard the real estate agent say the three most important things to remember in buying a home are . . . location, location, location. Well, I can summarize why most moms are working outside the home . . . financial, financial, financial. Under this broad financial umbrella, let's examine these reasons.

## 1. FINANCIAL NEED OR FINANCIAL WANT?

For most families, the decision for mom to work outside the home is due to financial reasons, which can range anywhere from real financial need to financial greed.

Some families literally could not survive financially without mom's working outside the home. The decision for some families is not a matter of, "Do we want to be able to drive a new car?" but, "Can we even afford to have one car for our family?" It's not about, "Do we want to go out for dinner tonight?" but, "Do we have food in the refrigerator to eat?"

However, most would agree that the majority of working moms would fall into the category of not really *having to work* but rather having made a *choice* to work.

Many families today are confusing *needs* with *wants*. In the prosperous culture in which we live, many things that are in reality

24

"wants" have been redefined as "needs." I challenge you to evaluate your "needs" based on the biblical definition found in 1 Timothy 6:6–8 (NASB, emphasis added), "But godliness actually is a means of great gain, when accompanied by contentment. For we have brought nothing into the world, so we cannot take anything out of it either. *If we have food and covering, with these we shall be content.*" Let the Word of God be your standard, not your neighbor.

Yes, some moms work because of real financial need, while others work simply out of financial want, but we would all have to agree that our tax system has contributed to many moms being forced to work outside the home. This leads us to reason 2.

## 2. Heavy Tax Burden

One reason both parents have to work is due to the financial pressures created by our federal, state, and local governments, not to mention the Social Security and Medicare taxes that are deducted from each paycheck. Just look at it from a dollars-and-cents perspective.

**Federal Taxes**

Let's assume a couple (with two children) is earning a combined income of $50,000. If you subtracted $7,350 for your standard deduction, and $11,200 for personal exemptions, your taxable income would be $31,450. Your taxes for the year would be $31,450 x 15% = $4,718. Your child tax credit of $1,000 would reduce your taxes to $3,718. This means that for every dollar you earn you will be paying 7.4% in taxes ($3,718 ÷ $50,000 = 7.44%). So, Mom, for every dollar that you earn, 7.4 cents goes to the federal government and you are allowed to keep 92.6 cents for the needs of your family. It would be fine if the taxes stopped here, but most families in America have to pay a state income tax.

**State Taxes**

Currently forty-four states have a state income tax. Let's assume after standard deductions you end up paying an average of 4 percent of your income to your state. Now, after paying federal and state taxes, you are left with 88.6 cents of every dollar you earn.

## Social Security and Medicare

Next we have to consider the deductions for Social Security and Medicare. The Social Security and Medicare tax of 15.3 percent is split equally between the employer and the employee. The employee's portion for Social Security and Medicare taxes amounts to 7.65 percent being deducted from your paycheck each month. Now you can keep 80.95 cents (88.6% - 7.65% = 80.95%) of every dollar you earn. I might also note that self-employed individuals have to pay the full 15.3 percent in taxes, because they are both the "employer" and the "employee." So, if you are self-employed, you are now down to 73 cents (88.6% - 15.3% = 73.3%). No wonder so few people can ever start a successfully run business of their own! For every $100 in earned income, they get to keep only $73.30!

## Sales Taxes

Let's not forget the sales tax that most of us pay. Only four states do not have a general sales tax on purchases. Let's assume the average sales tax is 6 percent (in many states it is much higher) on everything you purchase. But since you do not pay sales tax on things like your mortgage payment or charitable contributions, I will only use 4 percent for our rough calculations. Now you are keeping only 76.95 cents of every dollar you earn.

## Property Taxes

If you are a home owner, you will be paying property taxes. I realize that property taxes vary greatly, but let's assume our couple, earning $50,000, lives in a home valued at $85,000 and the city and county property taxes for the year will be a total of $1,000. This represents about 2 percent ($1,000 ÷ $50,000 = .02 or 2%) of their income going to pay property taxes. Now for every dollar you earn, you will be able to keep 74.95 cents (76.95% - 2% = 74.95%).

## Summary

Let's summarize what this looks like for our couple earning $50,000. For every dollar they earn . . .

7.40    cents goes to pay federal taxes
4.00    cents goes to pay state taxes

7.65 cents goes to pay Social Security and Medicare taxes (15.3 if self-employed)

4.00 cents goes to pay sales taxes

2.00 cents goes to pay property taxes

That adds up to 25.05 cents in taxes.

This couple would end up with 74.95 cents of every dollar they earn, and 25.05 cents goes just to pay taxes.

This means that if you earn a salary of $50,000, your family will end up with about $37,475 ($50,000 x 74.95% = $37,475) to live on, and $12,525 ($50,000 x 25.05% = $12,525) would go to pay taxes.

And, don't forget, the more income you earn, the higher the tax brackets. The above calculations were using the 15 percent tax bracket!

## Marriage Tax Penalty

Did you realize that our tax code even penalizes you for being married and filing a joint return? This aspect of the tax code has become known as the "Marriage Tax Penalty." Let's say that both the husband and wife are working and earning $30,000 each for a total income of $60,000. Compare this couple to two singles who are not married but are living together and each earning $30,000 for a total income of $60,000. Guess what? The unmarried couple living together receives the tax break. Therefore you are being financially penalized for being married. This issue continues to be debated in congress. A variety of bills are being introduced to address this problem, but none have been passed at the writing of this book. One bill reads, "To amend the Internal Revenue Code of 1986 to eliminate the marriage penalty by providing that the income tax rate bracket amounts, and the amount of the standard deduction, for joint returns shall be twice the amounts applicable to unmarried individuals."

## Tax Freedom Day

Did you realize that most Americans work until about May 10, just to earn enough to cover their federal, state, and local taxes? It has been called Tax Freedom Day. It seems as if every year they are having to add on a day or two due to the increased tax burden being placed on families.

By no means am I using this illustration to imply that our federal, state, and local governments should not tax their citizens. Our government needs income to operate, but I think most citizens believe that as a whole we are being over-taxed, government is spending too much, and families are being hurt!

Is the tax system the only reason so many moms have to work? No. But it is fair to say that this is a major contributor to the reason so many women have to work. Our next area discusses one of the most common reasons most moms work: excessive debt.

## 3. DEBT OBLIGATIONS

In addition to real financial needs and our burdensome tax structure, many families have amassed debt obligations that have forced both parents to work. I found it very interesting that Tina, Becky, and Traci all emphasized debt avoidance when Mary was interviewing them in chapter 2.

Tina said, "But we had tons of debt. We both had car payments at the time. I thought I would work for two years, and we would get the debt paid off." Four years later Tina is still working because of debt. Tina's advice to us: "Don't create any debt."

Becky's words of wisdom were, "Make that decision up front, and don't get in debt where you feel like you have to work."

Then we heard from Traci: "Whether or not you want to be a stay-at-home mom, do not accrue a lot of debt because you have to pay it back. If you do have kids and want to come home, it [debt] will make it more difficult."

Mom, if you are at home and want to stay there, listen to the wisdom of Tina, Becky, and Traci. If you are a working mom wanting to come home, then it is very likely that you could tell your own story about the real cost of debt—not just the financial cost from interest but the tougher cost, the one that cuts deep within your soul when you want to be home with your kids but just can't seem to ever get there.

## More Moms Working—More Family Debt

Now you figure this one out! More families have two people earning an income than ever before, yet credit card debt more than doubled in only seven years from 1989 ($210.9 billion) to 1996 ($498 billion). Remember, this is the same time frame that women accounted for 59 percent of labor-force growth.

## Automobile Debt Increasing

Automobile debt increased from $290.2 billion in 1986 to $390.3 billion in 1996.[1]

## Bankruptcy Increasing

Total bankruptcy filings are at an all-time high and have increased over 300 percent from 1982 (380,251) to 1996 (1,178,555).[2]

## The Stress of Repaying College Loans

In recent years I have noticed the tremendous burden being placed on young couples due to college loans they obtained while in school. Some young couples will be repaying those college loans for the next ten to twenty years. After seeing the financial stress these loans are placing on families, I have begun to counsel college students to consider seriously working their way through college or co-opt with a company. My friend Trenidy Davis had this to say about co-opt: "In my opinion, it's absolutely the best thing; it's the only way to do it. In many ways the work experience you receive is even better than the degree you receive. After I began working full-time, I did not start with an entry-level pay but with five years of experience, and that makes a big difference."

I can assure you, even if it takes an individual five or six years to finish college and remain debt-free, or have lower school loans, they will be better off emotionally and financially than if they finish college in four years and have accumulated debt to be repaid over the next twenty years.

In addition to the increased use of debt, we live in a very consumptive society. What it took many of our senior citizens thirty years to accomplish, many young couples want today! A beautiful house, a house full of new furniture, large-screen stereo television systems, not to mention the new cars and vans. For a lot of couples in America today, many of these purchases are obtainable only with the use of debt. Once the monthly debt obligations become so large, Mom has no option but to put the kids in child care, leave the home, and enter the job market–just to help make the minimum monthly payments. This added debt load is putting more financial pressure on the American family.

## 4. ISSUES OF LIFESTYLE AND SOCIAL PRESSURES

The issues of lifestyle can be closely tied to debt, but I believe they need to be addressed separately. Let's face it, the lifestyle you and I choose to live plays a major part in the decision of whether Mom is going to work outside the home. Mom may still have to work even if you pay cash for everything, if your lifestyle remains high!

Several years ago I remember one couple commenting that they used the wife's paycheck to cover the mortgage on their new house and to pay for child care. I thought to myself, *Well, if Mom stayed at home, they would not have the child-care expense.* And I wondered if they "really needed" to move into that new house? You and I know that all of our decisions come down to what we really value. Which do you value more, a bigger home or spending quality time with your children? I think you get the point.

The pressure to maintain a certain lifestyle can at times be overwhelming. I have talked with many couples or single moms over the years who don't even attend church because of the tremendous social pressure that is placed on them on Sunday mornings. Believe me, my heart goes out to these families.

Romans 12:1–2 (NASB) comes to mind as we address the issue of social pressures in life. It says, "I urge you therefore, brethren, by the mercies of God, to present your bodies a living and holy sacrifice, acceptable to God, which is your spiritual service of worship. And do not be conformed to this world, but be transformed by the renewing of your mind, that you may prove what the will of God is, that which is good and acceptable and perfect."

## 5. THE CAREER WOMAN

For some couples, moms working outside the home is not a matter of financial need or even want but a matter of career. Some women simply want to pursue a career, and remaining at home as a mom is just not part of their family plan. This became obvious to me when I was reading the responses to my "women's" survey (see chapter 4). A number of women made clear to me that they loved to work and had no intention of ever staying at home. You could almost sense that they were mad at me for even writing a book like this. Some of their notes were underlined, and you could tell they were writing with conviction! Once again, this book is not trying to convince anyone to do anything. I am simply trying to help those who want to be at home!

The heading of "career woman" reminds me of an Ann Landers article I read in the paper. See if this has a ring of truth to you:

Dear Ann Landers:
So you think "Dying Inside in the Midwest" needs antidepressants? That advice didn't sound like you, Ann. The woman has been working throughout her entire marriage. She's exhausted and wants to quit. She is just like every other working mother in America—worn out. Marriages today are business partnerships with sex. I was fortunate to be able to stay home when my children were young. I would not trade a single day of those years for any amount of money. I deeply regret that I was not at home when my children were teen-agers. I am sure we could have handled many problems better had I been there to nip them in the bud. My mother was a registered nurse and an officer during World War II. She never worked outside the home after she married. My father adored her. In the lean years, even if there was only oatmeal for supper, there was a clean tablecloth and cloth napkins on our laps. And what do I do? I go to meetings and take business trips. I spend eight to 10 hours a day at the office, and use my vacation days for

family emergencies. I haven't read a book just for fun in five years. There's never enough time for my kids, and I'm not alone. All of the working women I know will tell you the same story. Is there a way out?

Trapped by Success

Dear Trapped:

There IS a way out, but it means giving up something—a salary increase, a promotion, maybe the job itself. It is obvious that some women are paying too high a price for success. They should ask themselves, is it worth it? Your letter suggests it is not. Take a deep breath, review the options, and then do something about it.

Ann Landers[3]

This leads us to our last reason, and maybe the most important of all.

## 6. POOR MONEY MANAGEMENT

I am convinced that more moms who want to stay home really could with proper money management. Many families try to live on one income and fail because they are not living on a budget. I have devoted an entire chapter to budgeting. It's a simple plan called a MAP. A MAP is a Money Allocation Plan. You don't need a notebook with thirty-two tabs; all you need is one piece of paper each month! If you really desire to remain at home, using a MAP will be your road map to success!

It is amazing the amount of money that a family wastes by not living on a budget. And if you were to talk to most of these families, they would be quick to say, "But we never have enough." The key is to establish a plan for your money, then be disciplined to follow your plan and live within the boundaries you have established.

Let me give you one example: A number of years ago I counseled a couple having serious financial problems. After asking a few questions, I quickly determined that (1) they had no budget, (2) they had no real understanding of money management, and (3) they had absolutely no discipline when it came to spending money. I found out that the husband ate out for lunch everyday. I asked him, "How much do you spend on lunch?" He said, "Somewhere around $5 per day." So I simply said, "Let's do the math. Five dollars per day for five days is $25 per week. Twenty-five dollars per week for fifty-two weeks equals $1,300." Well, this couple's income was about $27,000 per year. So I explained that they were spending about 5 percent ($1,300 ÷ $27,000) of their income just for the husband to eat lunch. I recommended that he consider doing what I do most days and just take a sack lunch to the office. He was actually *offended* that I would make such a recommendation and left my office—never to return. His response showed spiritual, emotional, and financial immaturity.

One reason many moms who desire to stay at home cannot is because the husband and wife have never taken the time to develop a Money Allocation Plan (budget) and look for ways to cut their expenses. In three future chapters I will commit a considerable amount of space explaining how to evaluate your financial plan. You might need to explore the possibilities of moving to a less expensive house, driving a different car, planning your food budget better, and becoming more disciplined in managing your money.

## Looking Ahead

Now that we have examined the six primary reasons moms are working, we will begin to help you develop a plan to leave the marketplace and enter the home place. This process will involve communication exercises with your spouse, reaffirming your values, evaluating your goals, analyzing your present financial condition, and implementing a financial plan that will allow you to be at home with your children. After all, there's no place quite like it!

### Scripture to Ponder

"For this reason, since the day we heard about you, we have not stopped praying for you and asking God to fill you with the knowledge of his will through all spiritual wisdom and understanding" (Col. 1:9).

**Action Step**

You and your spouse (or a good friend of the same sex if you are not married) should jot down separately the top three things that you value in life. Share your findings and then compare your values with your calendar and checkbook. Discuss whether your actions support your values.

CHAPTER 4

# The Mom Survey

ETHAN

There are as many opinions as there are noses.

🐾 One Sunday morning I was a guest in a young married Sunday School class at my churchz. At this time no one knew I was working on this book. I was absolutely amazed that the most common prayer request concerned moms who wanted to be at home with their children or concerns about child-care problems. I just sat there and listened to these moms and dads as they poured out their frustrations and asked for prayer. After the class I asked my good friend and teacher of the class, Johnny Mayfield, if that prayer time was normal. He said, "Ethan, we hear requests like that on a regular basis." What I heard during that Sunday School class was confirmed by the results of my survey. A lot of moms are longing to leave the workplace and be at home with their children; they just don't know how they can financially accomplish it.

Let me begin by explaining how these surveys were taken. More than two hundred surveys were passed out in Sunday School classes to women of various ages and from a variety of states. Here is what they had to say. My commentary follows some of the questions:

## 1. Do you work outside your home?
**60% Yes            40% No**

These numbers reflect that the cultural norm has also become the Christian norm, since every survey was taken in Sunday School classes or a church environment. The same results would have been received if we went to the mall and took this survey.

**2. If yes, how much do you work?**
**72% Full-time     28% Part-time**

**3. Do you have children under the age of six?**
**53% Yes     47% No**

Fifty-three percent of these moms have children under the age of six. If there is any season of life when it would be best for a mom to be at home, it would have to be at this time.

**4. Do you have children seven to nineteen years old?**
**54% Yes     46% No**

**5. Did you grow up in a home with a working mom?**
**51% Yes     49% No**

It was interesting to correlate this question with question 1, "Do you work outside the home?" I wanted to see what percent of the working/nonworking moms surveyed had working/nonworking moms when they were growing up.

For those who *do not* work outside the home, 63 percent grew up in a home where mom did not work outside the home, while 37 percent grew up in a home with a working mom.

For those who *do* work outside the home, 58 percent had moms that worked outside the home, while 42 percent grew up in a home where mom did not work outside the home. So it appears that in *both cases* the mother definitely influenced the daughter in this area.

**6. If you are a working mom, would you like to be able to stay at home full-time if it were possible?**
**64% Yes     36% No**

These numbers do not surprise me, since many moms find fulfillment in a career outside the home.

**7. If you are a stay-at-home mom, would you like to be able to work outside the home?**
**7% Yes     93% No**

Based on these numbers, it appears that once mom gets to stay at home, she has no desire to leave! In fact, it appears that moms love to be home and find great fulfillment as stay-at-home moms.

8. **Would your husband agree with your answer to the above question?**

   **94% Yes**            **6% No**

Most of the husbands who would not agree with their wives have working wives, and they do not want them to quit work even if their wife's desire is to be at home.

Next I gave the moms a chance to express themselves beyond just a yes or no answer. Some direct quotes from the surveys are given in the following questions:

9. **If you work outside the home, what are the reasons?**

   | | |
   |---|---|
   | Finances and money issues | 77% |
   | Enjoy it, self-fulfillment in working | 14% |
   | A "calling" to teach, etc. | 5% |
   | Required to keep licenses, etc. | 2% |
   | Need to be around people | 2% |

Actual quotes taken from the surveys:
   "Financial needs."
   "To pay for private school."
   "My husband is out of work."
   "We need the money."
   "We have our own business, and I have to help out."
   "Braces and college."
   "I feel God led me to teach."
   "My husband is in medical school."
   "We are trying to pay off debt."
   "Purely financial, we cannot afford our lifestyle."
   "I enjoy it and need the extra income."
   "My husband requires it."
   "Fun."
   "I love my job."
   "I enjoy working. I feel like I am making a difference at my work."

"Social Security benefits and job experience."

"We need two incomes to support our family."

"Pay credit card bills."

"I like being around people."

**10. If you do not work outside your home, what are the reasons?**

| | |
|---|---|
| Family, children, home | 95% |
| Other reasons | 5% |

Actual quotes taken from the surveys:

"I believe the Lord wants me to be available to my family."

"To be there for my children and to watch them grow."

"I wanted to be able to raise my children during those impressionable years."

"To be home with my children."

"To be a full-time mother and wife."

"To be able to keep my children out of day care."

"To train my children in the ways of God."

"Child care would cost more than I could make."

"Manage our home."

"Because my kids and husband want me at home."

"My child is more important than the money."

"I homeschool my kids."

"I enjoy being at home."

"God has called me to spend 100 percent of my time at home."

"My husband and children are my first responsibility."

God's calling and the mom's desire to raise her children were definitely the most common responses to this question.

**11. If you do not work outside your home, what are some things you have had to give up in order to stay at home?**

Below you will find the list of what was on people's hearts when they filled out this survey. Most people listed more than one thing they had to give up. All the reasons were tabulated and the results are below.

| | |
|---|---|
| Extra money/spending money | 12% |
| Adult relationships/friendships at work | 12% |
| Nothing | 12% |
| Newer cars | 11% |
| Clothes | 11% |
| Eating out | 9% |
| Vacations/travel | 8% |
| Career | 7% |
| Bigger/new home | 3% |
| Independence | 2% |
| Gifts | 1% |
| Recreation vehicles | 1% |
| Clubs | 1% |
| My time | 1% |
| Other reasons combined | 9% |

Actual quotes taken from the surveys:

"Many material things."

"New cars."

"Clothes."

"Eating out."

"Vacations."

"Movies."

"Furniture."

"Bigger home."

"My career."

"Health club membership."

"More money."

"Appreciation/reward in the workplace."

"Adult interaction."

"Health benefits."

"I don't feel like I gave up anything; it's my job."

"Owning a home."

"Practically everything."

"Travel."

"Extra things for the kids."

"Simply going out to lunch with friends."

"Comfort level of our savings."

"Independence."

Now that we have looked at the hard data, let me try to summarize. I could have almost guessed what the results would be before I even surveyed these moms. But these results simply confirm what most of us already knew to be true.

## TWO MOST IMPORTANT ASPECTS OF ENTIRE SURVEY

1. This survey revealed that most moms who can stay at home don't want to leave. (See question 7.) I believe this is due to the overwhelming sense of fulfillment that comes from being at home.

2. The reason most moms feel they have to work is financial.

## A WORD TO ALL THE MOMS WHO PARTICIPATED IN THIS SURVEY

Let me thank all the moms who participated in this survey. I read every word, but most importantly I saw your heart. I really sensed the conviction many of you have about this area–whether to stay at home or to work outside the home. I could literally see the degree of conviction by the way you answered the questions. In many cases your writing was real bold or actually indented the paper! Wow! You helped me to understand why a book on this topic is so important. I never realized how deeply so many of you feel about this topic. After all, I'm just a dad. However, I believe that I will be a better husband and dad because of what you had to share with me. Thanks again for sharing your life with me.

I would like to close this chapter by sharing what one mom wrote on her survey. Since she filled up every available space on the front and back of the survey, it definitely caught my attention. Here was her message:

I feel so very strongly on this issue. Your children are purely and simply gifts from God, and they are given to you to nurture for a short time, not for another stand-in mom to bond with them at the most critical time—when they are babies until age five. All the child-care experts concur on this point. If you make the life-changing decision to have children, you should be ready and willing to set all other things aside to care for them. I can give you example after example of times God has provided for us when we could not buy groceries or pay a bill. We have prayed for help, and he has always come through. We have received numerous checks in the mail that were not expected and others that were expected and came exactly when they were needed. I have said all this simply to convey that a lot of people say they don't know how they would make it. We didn't either, but I was not willing to go to work full-time, and God has provided. Angelia Allen

Stay tuned, because in the chapters that follow, I will be giving solutions to help more moms, who want to be at home, get there and stay there!

**Scripture to Ponder**

"Brethren, I do not regard myself as having laid hold of it yet; but one thing I do: forgetting what lies behind and reaching forward to what lies ahead, I press on toward the goal for the prize of the upward call of God in Christ Jesus" (Phil. 3:13–14 NASB).

**Action Step**

Find another mom who desires to leave the workplace and form a prayer partnership. Begin to pray for each other every day. Press on toward your goal and calling.

CHAPTER 5

# Citizens of Earth or Bound for Heaven?

MARY

If you look past the world, you put your head up into eternity.

–Thomas Goodwin

🐾 Mom, if we could somehow pull back a curtain and show what is really inside us, what would we find? Do our thoughts and actions reveal women whose hearts long for the Savior? Do you and I consider ourselves to be permanent residents of earth or bound for heaven?

When earthly challenges would come for a friend of my husband's, this man would say, "Well, I am just passing through." How true that is! Philippians 3:20 tells us, "But our citizenship is in heaven."

Imagine yourself traveling to France or Italy. Before you leave the United States, you will have to go through the process of getting a passport that will show that you are an American citizen. When you pack, you bring only one or two suitcases. How silly it would be to transport all of your belongings to your vacation site. After all, you are only on a journey and will soon return home.

As you depart on a plane for your visit to another country, you choose a seat by the window. It's amazing how seemingly enormous buildings become no more than a speck as you climb higher and higher. You pass through the vapors of a cloud and find yourself surrounded by a sea of gorgeous clouds. Then you remember how you would lie in the grass as a child and gaze up at the sky–imagining the clouds to be huge mountains and fierce bears. And now you are actually flying in the midst of one of our Creator's finest masterpieces!

As you gaze from the plane at the specks of buildings below, suddenly your material possessions do not seem so important. Now massive skyscrapers seem like dots on a computer screen. And both mansions and shacks seem insignificant when compared to the vast space you are traveling through.

Mom, where's your true home? Is it in your city, on your block, in your house? Or, are you and I on a journey through life, bound for heaven. I think our perspective–how we look at life–makes all the difference in how we plan for life! And frankly, too often I think of home as the place where my family lives. I easily forget that I am really on a journey.

How we need to recognize the greatness of God in our everyday lives! I think we need to realize that our most important responsibility in life as mothers is to nurture the next generation and to train them in the ways of Jesus Christ! How does this mind-set affect our choices?

Jerry Bridges, former vice president for corporate affairs of the Navigators, wrote a wonderful book called *The Joy of Fearing God*.[1] I have drawn from his thoughts in creating the following chart:

## TIPS FOR A HEAVEN-BOUND MOM TO LIVE A GOD-FEARING LIFE

Acknowledgment    Lord, help me realize that every single thing that happens today is under your ultimate authority.

Submission    May I submit to the authority of Jesus Christ today and to those whom the Lord has placed in authority over me.

Awareness    Help me to be aware that wherever I am, God is there too.

| | |
|---|---|
| Trusting | Lord, may I trust you completely today, even when I just cannot see how you are working in my life. |
| Recognition | May I recognize that God can meet my needs in ways I cannot anticipate. |
| Dependence | Help me prayerfully depend on Jesus Christ to meet the needs of my family today. |
| Seeking | May I seek to live today to the glory of God. |
| Remember | May I remember that I own nothing. God is the ultimate owner of everything. |
| Worship | Lord, help me worship you in thought and attitude today—even when I am doing the most mundane task. What a privilege it is to worship you! |
| Enjoy | May I enjoy your presence today and not miss the truths you are revealing to me today. |

How different our plans look when we make decisions knowing that we are "just passing through." How different the day looks when we put God at the center of our thoughts and actions as did my friend Terri.

Not too long ago I witnessed Terri struggle with whether she should return to work as a school secretary while her youngest child was still at home. She had not solicited the job, and the call asking her to consider it was totally unexpected.

Terri had resigned as the school secretary when her youngest child, Jennifer, was born. It had been a perfect job for her family as her two sons attended the same Christian school where she worked. But Terri's mom had always told her, "Honey, you do not understand, and you will never know or be able to measure what your being at home builds into your children." Because of her mom's words and seeking God's will, Terri and her husband, Bill, decided that Terri should return home to be with her new infant.

But four years later, when college was looming on the horizon for their oldest son, the same job that Terri once had at the Christian school became open. When Terri was offered it, she wondered, *Could this be from the hand of God?*

As much as she wanted to accept the position and believe that it was from God, Terri had no peace and felt that it was being offered "a year or two too early." When an opening for Jennifer in the four-year-old class could not be made, Terri and Bill knew their answer: she would not accept the job.

"I tend to go on faith that God will provide some way—somehow," Terri says, "and sometimes his provisions are not monetary." She told me of the year when she and Bill decided to homeschool their son, Billy. Terri recalls, "It was a radical decision and made purely on finances. But during that year Billy and I began to understand each other and bond."

Terri continued, "God does not always answer our prayers by meeting our financial needs."

Terri and Bill have an eternity mind-set. Terri says, "I think God has worked a lot in our lives through financial distress and given us other blessings. I have learned not to rush things that look right. I want to do something because I feel a peace and know that it must be from God."

God has continued to show his faithfulness to Terri and her family this year. She is the school bus monitor (for the Christian school where her sons attend). This allows her to be with Jennifer on the bus and during the day, and it provides a discount on her sons' tuition.

Terri and Bill have modeled the verse, "Cast your cares on the LORD and he will sustain you" (Ps. 55:22). God has very tangibly shown his care for the Ruck family, and he has allowed Terri to invest time in her young daughter.

The Rucks recognize that the Lord regularly meets their needs in ways they cannot anticipate. They are like the boy in the poem below who also sees God in everyday life.

## WHERE GOD AIN'T
He was just a little lad,
and on the week's first day,

He was wandering home from Sunday school,
and dawdling on the day.
He scuffed his shoes into the grass;
he found a caterpillar;
He found a fluffy milkweed pod,
and blew out all the "filler."

A bird's nest in a tree o'er heard
so wisely placed on high,
Was just another wonder
that caught his eager eye.

A neighbor watched his zigzag course,
and hailed him from the lawn;
Asked him where he'd been that day,
and what was going on.

"I've been to Bible school," he said,
and turned a piece of sod.
He picked up a wiggly worm and said,
"I've learned a lot of God."

"M'm a very fine way," the neighbor said,
"for a boy to spend his time."
"If you'll tell me where God is,
I'll give you a brand new dime."

Quick as a flash his answer came!
Nor were his accents faint.
"I'll give you a dollar, Mister,
if you tell me where God ain't!"

—Author Unknown

Mom, I think there is so much truth in this little poem. God is all around us. His power, his majesty, his glory just shouts from nature. If this is so, why do we so often not hear? I don't know about you, but sometimes I am just not listening.

*Lord, help us to be moms whose hearts are bound for heaven and whose actions on earth point our children to Jesus Christ.*

**Scriptures to Ponder**

"And my God will meet all your needs according to his glorious riches in Christ Jesus" (Phil. 4:19).

"Show me, O Lord, my life's end and the number of my days; let me know how fleeting is my life" (Ps. 39:4).

**Action Steps**

1. How does your lifestyle reveal that you are a heaven-bound mom living a God-fearing life?

2. Write a prayer below asking God to help you focus on him and his truths. For the next week, record below specific truths that he reveals to you.

## CHAPTER 6

# Your Road Map Home—A Five-Step Plan to Get You Home (1)

## ETHAN

*Sacrifice: The act of giving up or forgoing something valued for the sake of something having a more pressing claim.*

 The next three chapters are devoted to helping you develop a workable financial plan to make it possible for you to move from the workplace to the home place. This is where we will begin the process of moving from the desire or dream to the real-life; "here's what it is going to take" to do it! Look at the process from this perspective:

Thought
↓
Dream
↓
Desire
↓
Conviction
↓
Evaluation
↓
Plan
↓
Implementation

Let's assume that you are presently at the conviction stage, and you are 100 percent sure that you want to move from the workplace to the home place. Your next step will be to evaluate where you are financially, develop your plan, and finally implement your plan!

If your goal is to stay at home, then you must develop a plan to accomplish your goal, or it is very likely you will never accomplish your goal. It will only remain a frustrating dream resulting in eventual disappointment for the rest of your life. "Hope deferred makes the heart sick, But desire fulfilled is a tree of life" (Prov. 13:12 NASB).

The further along you are in processing your decision, the greater the frustration you will experience if you do not accomplish your goal. For example, if staying at home is only a passing thought, your level of frustration may only be a 1 or 2 on a scale of 1 to 10. However, if you have reached the conviction level, and you believe it is the right thing for you to do, your level of frustration and anxiety might be a 9 or 10.

| Where You Are | Level of Frustration |
|---|---|
| Thought | 1–3 |
| Dream | 4–5 |
| Desire | 6–8 |
| Conviction | 9–10 |

Let me go ahead and prepare you. The evaluation, planning, and implementation are not going to be easy assignments for you to complete. However, be assured that my heart and prayers go out to you as you seek to be obedient to God's calling in your life. Nothing is greater than knowing Jesus as your Savior and being in the center of his will for your life. Your assignment in this chapter is going to require prayer, hard work, hours of communication with your spouse, soul-searching, probably the shedding of a few tears, and a personal appointment with God!

You could be facing some of the most difficult decisions in your entire life. I am confident that the word *sacrifice* will take on a whole new meaning in your life. The word *sacrifice* means "the act of giving up or forgoing something valued for the sake of something having a more pressing claim."

Most families who move from two incomes to one will be giving up things like newer cars, bigger homes, more furniture, and nicer clothes—but all for a greater calling! Is being at home with your family worth the sacrifice? Only you can answer this question. I trust that because you are reading this book the answer is *yes*.

There are times in life when we need to set aside the things that might entangle us and run the race that has been set before us. "Therefore, since we have so great a cloud of witnesses surrounding us, let us also lay aside every encumbrance, and the sin which so easily entangles us, and let us run with endurance the race that is set before us, fixing our eyes on Jesus, the author and perfecter of faith, who for the joy set before Him endured the cross, despising the shame, and has sat down at the right hand of the throne of God" (Heb. 12:1–2 NASB).

## A WORD OF ENCOURAGEMENT

Now let me give you a word of encouragement. When you finish your assignments in these three chapters and get all the financial details worked out so that you will be able to stay at home, I am confident that your soul will be shouting for joy and you will feel an overwhelming sense of peace and contentment in your life that can only come from God. You will have counted the cost and paid the price, and your family will be eternally grateful for your daily investment in their lives!

Let me begin by giving you an overview of how I believe you can establish a workable plan for your family. I will be using an acrostic of the word PLANS to teach you the process:

| | |
|---|---|
| **P** | Prepare spiritually. |
| **L** | List your priorities. |
| **A** | Analyze your finances. |
| **N** | Negotiate your solutions. |
| **S** | Start using your MAP: Money Allocation Plan. |

## PREPARE SPIRITUALLY

I believe the best place to begin any planning process is with prayer. Pray and ask the God of the universe to give you spiritual wisdom as you work your way through this process. "But if any of you lacks wisdom, let him ask of God, who gives to all men generously and without reproach, and it will be given to him" (James 1:5 NASB). Develop the attitude that nothing is impossible with God!

What you don't need is more wisdom from the world. "For the wisdom of this world is foolishness before God" (1 Cor. 3:19 NASB). Nor should you be asking natural men (those who do not know Christ) for their wisdom. "But a natural man does not accept the things of the Spirit of God; for they are foolishness to him, and he cannot understand them, because they are spiritually appraised" (1 Cor. 2:14 NASB).

Nor should you be basing your plan or decisions on the pattern of this world. "And do not be conformed to this world, but be transformed by the renewing of your mind, that you may prove what the will of God is, that which is good and acceptable and perfect" (Rom. 12:2 NASB). In other words, don't base your plans on what your neighbor is doing, but spend time in prayer and reading God's Word, in order to determine what is good and acceptable and perfect for your family.

Finally, as you begin prayerfully to consider your plan, be prepared for spiritual warfare. You might be thinking, *Come on Ethan, this is a financial issue, not a spiritual issue.* Friend, I can assure you that this battle begins on your knees and will be won on your knees. Be spiritually prepared for Satan to throw everything in his arsenal at you. As you are establishing your new budget, sacrificing, and cutting back your expenses, I can assure you that your friends and neighbors will be buying new cars, moving to larger homes, going on ski trips, and walking into church wearing new clothes every Sunday. However, you must be courageous and confident in your calling and keep your eyes fixed on Jesus!

Satan will try to use the circumstances around you to discourage you and simply have you give up. But you shall rise up every morning and "put on the full armor of God, that you may be able to stand firm against the schemes of the devil" (Eph. 6:11 NASB). "Your adversary, the devil, prowls around like a roaring lion, seeking someone to devour. But resist him, firm in your faith, knowing that the same experiences of suffering are being accomplished by your brethren who are in the world. And after you have suffered for a little while, the God of all grace, who called you to His eternal glory in Christ, will Himself perfect, confirm, strengthen and establish you. To Him be dominion forever and ever. Amen" (1 Pet. 5:8–11 NASB).

Do not be deceived. The issues we are dealing with are not just financial; they are also issues of the spirit and the heart. Be sure that you are prepared spiritually, before you begin to address the financial issues in your life and family.

Finally, as you are developing your financial plan, let me encourage you to read and meditate on the following passages for the next thirty days. Take one new passage every day. Maybe you will want to write it out on a three-inch by five-inch card and carry it with you through the day and eventually post it on your bathroom mirror. Ask God to use his Word to give you wisdom, strength, courage, and conviction as you begin your transition.

Let me encourage you not to skip this 30–day exercise and blessing!

1. Habakkuk 3:17–19
2. 1 Chronicles 4:10
3. 2 Chronicles 16:9
4. 2 Corinthians 12:9–10
5. Zechariah 4:6
6. Micah 6:8
7. Esther 4:14
8. Joshua 1:8
9. Psalm 1:1–6
10. Psalm 23:1–6

11. Psalm 34:1
12. Psalm 34:10, 18
13. Psalm 37:1–7
14. Psalm 51:10–12
15. Psalm 127:1–5
16. Psalm 135:15–18
17. Psalm 139:23–24
18. Proverbs 3:5–8
19. Proverbs 17:1
20. Jeremiah 29:11–13
21. Jeremiah 33:3
22. Matthew 6:19–34
23. Matthew 7:24–27
24. 1 Corinthians 2:14; 3:19
25. Galatians 5:16–26
26. Ephesians 5:15–20
27. Ephesians 6:10–18
28. Philippians 4:6–8
29. Philippians 4:11–13
30. Colossians 2:8

## List Your Priorities

Now that you have prepared yourself spiritually, the second aspect in developing your plan is to develop a list of your priorities. What are your real priorities in life? Have you ever taken the time to sit down with your spouse and write your priorities on a piece of paper? Your written priorities will help you determine how you spend your time and your money.

Is having mom at home with the kids really a priority or just a passing thought or dream? Is staying at home your goal because some of your friends are staying at home and it seems like the right thing to do, or is it a conviction and goal that you are so willing to accomplish that you are willing to make sacrifices like never before in your life? I propose if it is really a high priority or conviction, you will do anything in the world, including material sacrifices, to make it a reality. However, if it is simply a passing thought, I propose that it will never happen. Don't keep on kidding yourself year after year. Wake up and face reality.

Mary earlier shared the illustration about setting priorities–using a glass jar and big rocks. Let me ask you, what are the big rocks (priorities) you would put into the jar first? What would your spouse put into the jar first? Would you both be putting the same rocks (priorities) into the jar, or would each of your jars be full of different large rocks (priorities). In order for any mom to be able to stay at home, both spouses need to be sure they are putting the same large rocks (mom staying at home) into the jar. Otherwise, I can guarantee you it will never work.

What are the five most important priorities in your life? Go ahead and quickly jot them down. What is important in your life? Ask your spouse to do the same (before he/she sees your list).

Now you and your spouse (if you are married) should write down your priorities.

You have correctly stated your priorities if you are spending considerable time and money to accomplish them. Or, I might add, if you have made financial sacrifices because of them.

Now take some considerable time and look at them. Are these the priorities that you really want to have? Which ones do you need to change, if any?

This list should help you determine how you will be spending your time and your money. Be sure you and your spouse have carefully determined the priorities for your family before you move on to the next area.

By the way, I define a *priority* as something that is important to you and is reflected in your life every day by how much time you devote to it and to the degree that you are willing to let it affect your financial decisions in life. The higher the priority the more you will be willing to devote time to it and the more it will affect your checkbook.

Let me give you a simple example. I have nothing against bird watchers, but watching birds is absolutely not a priority in my life. On a scale of 1 to 10, it would score a minus 5. I am not going to take a perfectly good weekend and spend Saturday driving hundreds of miles and spend good money to try to find a rare bird singing in the top of a tree. About the most excited I have ever gotten about birds is when I saw our calico cat (Prancer) literally jump about five feet off the ground while trying to catch a bird as he flew over her head. Bird watching is just not a priority in my life.

However, if my daughter is in a piano competition on a Saturday, I will gladly drive hours in the car, spend the entire day cheering for her, and use our financial resources to pay for her piano lessons, music, entry fee, gasoline, and food expenses. You see, my daughter is a priority in my life, and I have invested the time and money to prove it. Just for the record, the same would be true if my son were playing in a tennis tournament or my wife was speaking at a conference!

Remember, the true test of a priority is many times based on time and money.

If you aren't quite sure what your priorities in life really are, just ask your spouse or better yet, pull out your calendar and checkbook!

Here is where I am headed with this point. Is having Mom at home a true priority so that you are willing to sacrifice time and money, or is it just a nice dream?

In this chapter we have covered the first two steps of a five-part plan to get you home where you want to be: (1) prepare spiritually and (2) list your priorities. In chapter 7, we will take a look at (3) how to analyze your finances and (4) negotiate your solutions. And in chapter 8 you will find out (5) how to implement your plan by using a Money Allocation Plan.

**Scripture to Ponder**

"Hope deferred makes the heart sick, but a longing fulfilled is a tree of life" (Prov. 13:12).

**Action Steps**

1. Meditate on the thirty Bible passages suggested in this chapter during the next thirty days.

2. List your top priorities on a piece of paper.

CHAPTER 7

# Your Road Map Home—A Five-Step Plan to Get You Home (2)

### ETHAN

> But seek first His kingdom and His righteousness;
> and all these things shall be added to you.
> —Matthew 6:33 NASB

Once you are spiritually prepared and determined that having Mom at home is a real priority, your next step is to analyze your finances. But before we move on to the next two areas of our plan, let's have a quick review:

**P**  Prepare spiritually (chapters 5 and 6).

**L**  List your priorities (chapter 6).

**A**  Analyze your finances (chapter 7).

**N**  Negotiate your solutions (chapter 7).

**S**  Start using your MAP: Money Allocation Plan (chapter 8).

## ANALYZE YOUR FINANCES

Don't even consider skipping this section because proper financial analysis serves as the foundation to your successful financial plan. Without a good foundation you are simply building on shifting sand.

If you are looking to move from two salaries to one or to keep living on one income, you will need to establish how much income you have to work with and how much your expenses are going to be each month.

## INCOME PROJECTION

The first step is to determine how much income you can expect to be receiving each month (with and without the wife working). On the work sheet that follows, or on another piece of paper, list your sources of income.

## EXPENSE PROJECTION

Next you will need to determine carefully how much your expenses have been each month. You will need to divide annual expenses by 12, semiannual expenses by 2, and quarterly expenses by 3. For example, if your home property taxes are $1,200 per year, your monthly allocation need would be $100 per month ($1,200 ÷ 12 = $100).

This work sheet will take considerable time and effort on your part, but it will be well worth the effort once you have finished. It will be impossible for you to realistically determine if Mom can move from the workplace to the home place without knowing this information. In fact, it would be foolish for Mom to stop working if it is financially impossible to pay the current obligations. Maybe you will need to make some changes before you stop working, or maybe you will determine that you can make it financially, even if you stop working today!

Spend some time working on the following information. You might need to go back in the checkbook for six months to obtain some realistic figures. The amounts you write down below are only as good as their source. Be sure you do your research and not just guess at the numbers.

First, you will find a sample work sheet filled out for you to examine. Notice how the income dropped $1,388 per month ($16,656 per year) and how various expenses had to be decreased accordingly. Don't get bogged down analyzing this example. Spend your time working on your personal income and expenses.

## SAMPLE WORK SHEET
## MONTHLY INCOME

| Sources of Income | Actual With Mom Working | Projected With Mom at Home |
|---|---|---|
| Joe's Income | $2,412 | $2,412 |
| Susan's Income | $1,388 | $0 |
| Total | $3,800 | $2,412 |

## SAMPLE WORK SHEET
## MONTHLY EXPENSES

| | Actual With Mom Working | Projected With Mom at Home | Notes |
|---|---|---|---|
| **Giving** | | | |
| Church | $380 | $250 | (Don't cut back on giving–still giving 10%.) |
| **Saving** | | | |
| Emergency Fund | $145 | $100 | (Can't save as much now, but this is OK.) |
| Retirement | $_____ | $_____ | |
| College | $_____ | $_____ | |
| _____ | $_____ | $_____ | |
| **Housing** | | | |
| Mortgage/Rent | $600 | $600 | (Living in same house) |
| Insurance | $30 | $30 | Pretty much same |
| Taxes | $60 | $60 | fixed expenses. |
| Electricity | $65 | $65 | Some families might |
| Gas/Heat | $30 | $30 | need to sell house to |
| Water | $20 | $20 | lower expenses. |
| Cable TV | $30 | $7 | Limited basic cable |

| | | | |
|---|---|---|---|
| Telephone | $55 | $40 | Fewer long-distance calls |
| Repairs | $50 | $50 | |
| _____ | $_____ | $_____ | |
| **Food** | | | |
| Grocery Store | $450 | $400 | Use coupons |
| Meals Out | $100 | $50 | Eat out less |
| Children | $_____ | $_____ | |
| **Debt Repayment** | | | |
| Credit Cards | $165 | $0 | Paid off before Mom |
| School Loans | $100 | $0 | stopped working |
| **Insurance** | | | |
| Life | $50 | $50 | |
| Health | $_____ | $_____ | |
| _____ | $_____ | $_____ | |
| **Car** | | | |
| Car Payment/Savings | $200 | $0 | Car paid in full |
| Insurance | $50 | $40 | Older car |
| Gasoline | $100 | $100 | |
| Maint. & Repairs | $50 | $50 | |
| **Social** | | | |
| Baby-sitting | $_____ | $_____ | |
| Children | $_____ | $_____ | |
| Vacations | $_____ | $_____ | |
| _____ | $_____ | $_____ | |
| **Clothing** | | | |
| _____ | $200 | $100 | Had to cut back |
| _____ | $_____ | $_____ | |
| _____ | $_____ | $_____ | |
| _____ | $_____ | $_____ | |
| **Child Care** | | | |
| ABC Daycare | $500 | $0 | Mom's at home! |
| _____ | $_____ | $_____ | |

House cleaning (maid)

| | | |
|---|---|---|
| _____ | $_____ | $_____ |
| _____ | $_____ | $_____ |

Medical

| | | |
|---|---|---|
| Dental | $50 | $50 |
| Doctor/Hospital | $_____ | $_____ |

Personal Allowance

| | | |
|---|---|---|
| Husband | $50 | $50 |
| Wife | $50 | $50 |
| _____ | $_____ | $_____ |

Household

| | | |
|---|---|---|
| Misc. Items | $50 | $50 |
| _____ | $_____ | $_____ |

Gifts

| | | |
|---|---|---|
| Birthday | $30 | $30 |
| Christmas | $25 | $25 |
| Wedding/Shower | $5 | $5 |
| Anniversary | $5 | $5 |
| Baby | $5 | $5 |

Education

| | | |
|---|---|---|
| College | $_____ | $_____ |
| _____ | $_____ | $_____ |

Misc.

| | | |
|---|---|---|
| _____ | $100 | $100 |

| | | |
|---|---|---|
| **TOTAL EXPENSES** | **$3,800** | **$2,412** |

The difference of $1,388 per month is due to the fact that Mom is no longer working.

## YOUR WORK SHEET
## MONTHLY INCOME

| Income<br>Sources of Income | Actual<br>With Mom<br>Working | Projected<br>With Mom<br>at Home |
|---|---|---|
| _____ | $_____ | $_____ |
| _____ | $_____ | $_____ |
| _____ | $_____ | $_____ |
| Total | $_____ | $_____ |

## YOUR WORK SHEET
## MONTHLY EXPENSES

| | Actual<br>With Mom<br>Working | Projected<br>With Mom<br>at Home |
|---|---|---|
| **Giving** | | |
| Church | $_____ | $_____ |
| _____ | $_____ | $_____ |
| _____ | $_____ | $_____ |
| **Saving** | | |
| Emergency Fund | $_____ | $_____ |
| Retirement | $_____ | $_____ |
| College | $_____ | $_____ |
| _____ | $_____ | $_____ |
| **Housing** | | |
| Mortgage/Rent | $_____ | $_____ |
| Insurance | $_____ | $_____ |
| Taxes | $_____ | $_____ |
| Electricity | $_____ | $_____ |
| Gas/Heat | $_____ | $_____ |
| Water | $_____ | $_____ |
| Cable TV | $_____ | $_____ |
| Telephone | $_____ | $_____ |

Repairs                      $_____        $_____
_____             $_____        $_____

Food
   Grocery Store             $_____        $_____
   Meals Out                 $_____        $_____
   Children                  $_____        $_____

Debt Repayment
_____             $_____        $_____
_____             $_____        $_____

Insurance
   Life                      $_____        $_____
   Health                    $_____        $_____
   _____                  $_____        $_____

Car
   Car Payment/Savings       $_____        $_____
   Insurance                 $_____        $_____
   Gasoline                  $_____        $_____
   Maint. & Repairs          $_____        $_____
   _____          $_____        $_____

Social
   Baby-sitting              $_____        $_____
   Children                  $_____        $_____
   Vacations                 $_____        $_____
   _____          $_____        $_____

Clothing
   _____          $_____        $_____
   _____          $_____        $_____
   _____          $_____        $_____
   _____          $_____        $_____

Child Care
   _____          $_____        $_____
   _____          $_____        $_____

House cleaning (maid)

| | | |
|---|---|---|
| _____ | $_____ | $_____ |
| _____ | $_____ | $_____ |

Medical
   Dental $_____     $_____
   Doctor/Hospital $_____     $_____

Personal Allowance

| | | |
|---|---|---|
| _____ | $_____ | $_____ |
| _____ | $_____ | $_____ |
| _____ | $_____ | $_____ |

Household
   Misc. Items $_____     $_____
   _____ $_____     $_____

Gifts
   Birthday $_____     $_____
   Christmas $_____     $_____
   Wedding/Shower $_____     $_____
   Anniversary $_____     $_____
   Baby $_____     $_____

Education
   College $_____     $_____
   _____ $_____     $_____

Misc.
   _____ $_____     $_____

**TOTAL EXPENSES**     **$_____**     **$_____**

Once you have determined your expenses and calculated the grand total, see if your expenses exceed your projected income, or does your income exceed your projected expenses? If you are like most families, your projected expenses will exceed your projected income. If this is true, now you will need to spend considerable time deciding which expenses you can cut in order for your budget to balance.

If one income is not going to be enough to cover your expenses, you might consider some of the following options:

- Begin a home-based business to help supplement your income needs.
- Consider part-time employment or working on weekends.
- Take care of the children for another family to earn income.
- Move to a less expensive home or apartment.

## NEGOTIATE YOUR SOLUTIONS

Now comes the time for husband and wife to negotiate cutbacks and find reasonable ways to decrease expenses. Maybe the family is accustomed to eating out several times a week, but if Mom is going to stay home, the family might need to sacrifice this luxury. You will need to go back and carefully analyze each expense. For each line item, ask the following questions:

1. Is this a necessity or a desire?
2. Can this expense be totally eliminated?
3. Can this expense be decreased in any way?

Your goal is to be sure that your planned expenses do not exceed your planned income.

Listed below you will find a brief financial commentary on each budget category.

**Income**

If you are moving from two incomes to just one, you will need to be sure that in reality you can live on just one income. Mom, before you turn in your resignation and kiss the office good-bye, try to live on just one income for at least six months. If you cannot do it, naturally you will need to make some adjustments in your budget. If you see that the one income is not going to be enough, you have two options: try to find ways to increase the one income or find additional ways to decrease your expenses.

**Giving**

This is one area where you want to remain faithful. Don't rob God! If you are not generously supporting God's kingdom, you need to begin. I am convinced that if you are faithful in supporting his kingdom, God can take what is left over and multiply it for your family. I can assure you, the God who called you to come home is the same God who does not want you to become a token giver. Going home is a step of financial faith; in the same way, giving is a step of faith.

Maybe you will be giving less, due to having only one income, but God only calls us to give out of what we receive. Let's assume that on two incomes you were earning $50,000 and supporting God's kingdom $5,000 per year ($50,000 x 10% = $5,000), but now your family is earning only $36,000. If you tithe, your giving will become $3,600 ($36,000 x 10% = $3,600). I would strongly encourage you to remain faithful in your giving, even if you are eliminating half of your income. God will honor your faithfulness! (Mal. 3:8–10). Read also 2 Corinthians 8:1–5.

**Saving**

Even with a reduced budget you still need to have some money being set aside in savings. If you have no savings, you will be forced to use credit cards when you incur a major car repair, house repair, or medical bill. You must have an emergency fund of at least one to three months' salary set aside. In fact, it will be very possible to have one to three months' salary set aside in an emergency fund if Mom is still working for the next six months (but you are living on one income). If you are moving from two incomes to one, it is likely you will not be able to save as much (if any) for college expenses or retirement. Let me encourage you not to trade saving for retirement needs for spending time with your children while they are young. Which would you rather have, one million dollars in the bank at age sixty and no real relationship with your children, or limited resources but a rich relationship with your children that will last for eternity?

**Housing**

For most families' housing tends to be the largest expense category, consuming anywhere from 20 to 50 percent of your take-home pay. If you are having to use over 40 percent for your total housing expenses, maybe you will need prayerfully to consider moving your family to a smaller or less expensive home in order to accomplish your goal of getting Mom home.

I realize this would be a hard thing for most families to do, but in reality this action just might be the only way you can achieve your goal to stay at home full-time. If you are buying your first home or a new home, be sure you use only one income to qualify for the mortgage.

Janet and I downsized our home in order to decrease our expenses. This was one of the hardest decisions in my life, but it was the right thing to do. We literally sold our nice two-story redbrick home while we were living in Richardson, Texas, and purchased a home that had been on the market for over two years. The purchase price was approximately 46 percent of the house we had sold just a few weeks earlier. I assume that most would agree that this was a significant cutback. After walking through the home once, Janet and I realized why no one wanted to purchase it. I will spare you all the specific details, but for example, the den had black paint on the walls and black shag carpet. After ripping out all the carpet, painting every inch of the interior and exterior (three coats) from top to bottom, refinishing the hardwood floors, and updating the kitchen, it really turned into a very lovable, cute, warm home for our growing family. Natalie was four at this time, and Austin was two. We have many precious memories of our family in this house. I still have pictures in my scheduling notebook of Natalie and Austin playing in our swimming pool (which was one foot deep and four feet wide). Moving from our larger two-story house to a smaller house, we looked like a failure to many, but I believe that God was sitting in heaven smiling at his children.

I do not know God's will for your life, but I do know that it took a major housing change in order for us to cut our expenses and for Janet to remain at home.

## Mortgage

It might be possible for you to remain in your present home but simply refinance your mortgage. If interest rates are at least 2 percent lower than your present home mortgage rate, you should check into refinancing your home. However, be sure you plan to live in your home long enough to cover your refinancing costs.

## Cable TV

Another thing we did was to eliminate the cable TV bill. To be honest it was great. I can assure you we spent more time together as a family because we did not have cable TV. Some cities offer limited basic cable. It is not basic, but limited basic. Generally, you will never see it advertised, but some states require cable companies to offer it. In our city it is $5.95 per month. Typically you get the four major networks, one religious channel, one weather channel, CNN Headline News, but it does not include things like ESPN. It really is limited basic!

## Telephone

Check and be sure you are with a company that offers the best long-distance rates. Rates are becoming more competitive every day. Also, you might need to work at limiting your long-distance calls to help you save money. A great option for communication has become E-mail. If you have access to the Internet, it will literally cost you nothing to send and receive E-mail. If you really need to save money, be sure you eliminate all the features on your bill like call waiting, call forwarding, and caller ID. Just sign up for the basic plan.

Cell phones have become a major expense for many families. I recently talked to one friend who is spending anywhere from $60 to $100 per month for his cell phone. Maybe using a cell phone has become a way of life for you, but the elimination of a cell phone might have to be one of your sacrifices.

## Home Repairs

Maybe being a handyman is not your dream, but in order to cut expenses you might need to learn a few basic skills in plumbing, carpentry, and painting. It will always cost less for you to do your own repairs. You should also consider attending free how-to seminars at your local Home Depot or Lowe's building supply store. You can learn how to wallpaper, install lighting fixtures, fans, shower enclosures, ceramic tile floors, and build a wood deck—just to name a few.

## Utilities

You might need to do a better job of controlling the thermostat during the day.

## Home Insurance

Talk with your agent about increasing your home owners insurance deductible to help lower your premium.

## Food

Cutting back on eating out and becoming a smart shopper can have a radical impact on your food budget. Plan your meals and make smart shopping trips to the store. Many people don't like coupons, but they can save a bundle over a year's time. For example, if you save $10 per week, that's more than $500 a year. This could be a lot of money to a family who is living on one income now.

## Eating Out

This is one area where most families will have to cut back. Even eating out three to six times a month could cost more than $100, or $1,200 per year. Let me encourage you to track carefully how much you spend eating out during the next four weeks.

## Child Care

For working moms with small children, the cost of child care can be very expensive, as you know. The good news is, if you are now staying at home, your child care expenses should be completely eliminated. This should be a great help to the family budget.

## Debt Repayment

This could be the one category that will keep moms in the workplace longer than expected. Due to the accumulation of school loans, credit card debts, car payments, and other debts, some moms will have to continue working until these loans are paid in full. Make debt repayment a high priority in your budget.

**Transportation**

Be creative in looking for ways to cut your expenses. Consider buying used cars instead of new cars. Talk to your car insurance agent about lowering your premium by increasing your deductible. Talk to your neighbors about carpooling to school or work.

**Health Insurance**

Do not risk going for one day without health insurance! With the cost of medical care, this is one area you cannot eliminate. Make sure you have adequate life insurance, but be careful you are not overinsured! Always carefully compare rates for all your insurance needs. Don't just pay the premium when it arrives; go ahead and call three other companies for comparable quotes.

**Social**

Be creative in this area! Instead of the family spending $25 going to a new movie release, consider renting a video for $3 and make some microwave popcorn at home. Some families save tons of money by camping out close to the beach or mountains (as opposed to staying at a hotel), and they actually enjoy it. However, I have yet to convince my wife that camping out is fun!

**Clothing**

Another area of expense for working moms is clothing. You should be able to cut back in this area if you are not working outside the home. In many cases the elimination of child care expenses, decrease in clothing expenses, and the decrease in car expenses can almost make up for the loss of your income due to the fact you have stopped working.

Be sure you are operating on a specific clothing budget, and don't overspend it. Try to find the great sales and good values. Most of us on a limited budget cannot afford to buy $125 tennis shoes but must settle for the $45 no-name brand. By the way, they wear just as well. Buying nonbrands might be one of the ways your family will need to sacrifice. Shopping at outlet malls, even for brand names, is a great way to save money.

**Medical**

If you are paying for your own health insurance, one way to decrease your monthly expenses is to have your deductible increased. For example, a monthly health insurance premium with a $250 annual deduction for a family of four might cost $600 per month. By increasing the deductible to $1,000 the monthly cost might drop the premium to $400 per month–for a savings of $200 per month. Do you think you will be spending more than $200 per month in doctor visits and prescriptions? If not, this might be a good way to lower your expenses.

**Allowances**

Everyone needs to have a personal allowance, even if it is small. Your personal allowance money is used for things personal to you and not necessarily for the entire family.

**Gifts**

Most families going from two incomes to one will usually have a significant decrease in their gift category. Once again, establish an amount to spend and do not exceed it. Maybe in large families, or extended families, you might consider drawing names instead of buying every person a present. Give cards instead of gifts.

**Miscellaneous**

This is the category you will need to plan for carefully and monitor. Be sure you adequately fund this category, or you will find it to be a real budget buster.

**Conclusion**

Go over your planned expenses line by line and evaluate each and every one!

Your goal is to create a MAP (budget) that works for you. Once you believe that you have a workable MAP using one income, be sure you live on it for at least six months to be sure it will work. It is better to find out it is not workable while Mom is still earning an income than to have her quit her job and place your family in a potential financial crisis.

There is no magical or simple formula to make this procedure easy. Projecting your monthly living expenses is a time-consuming task but well worth the effort.

In the next chapter I will teach you the final aspect of your plan, using the Money Allocation Plan.

## SUMMARY

**P**     Prepare spiritually.

**L**     List your priorities.

**A**     Analyze your finances.

**N**     Negotiate your solutions.

**S**     Start using your MAP: Money Allocation Plan.

**Scripture to Ponder**

"The plans of the diligent lead surely to advantage, But everyone who is hasty comes surely to poverty" (Prov. 21:5 NASB).

**Action Steps**

Follow the guidelines in this chapter and:

1. Analyze your finances.

2. Negotiate your solutions.

CHAPTER 8

# Your MAP to Success—Using the Money Allocation Plan

ETHAN

*For which one of you, when he wants to build a tower, does not first
sit down and calculate the cost, to see if he has enough to complete it?*
—Luke 14:28 NASB

Now that you have established your plan (chapters 6 and 7), I
am convinced the long-term key to your success will be based on
how you manage your money on a daily basis, and this will require
that you operate on a budget. Just by mentioning the word *budget*, I
can already tell that your blood pressure is rising and thoughts of
bondage, frustration, and stress are immediately coming to mind. Just
relax. Stop right now, make yourself a cup of coffee or a large bowl
of ice cream, and let's talk. First, let's both agree to stop using the B
word and begin using the word MAP, Money Allocation Plan.

I know that it is hard to believe, but a MAP does not have to be
stressful! If you find the right one for you, it can be one of the most
freeing things you have ever done. My friend Karl Ficken said that
before his family started using a MAP, he used to come home, look
at the checkbook, get all upset, and grumble about how much money
"his wife" was spending. However, since they have been operating on
a MAP, life is much calmer. I might add that his wife, Kay, agrees 100
percent!

There are a lot of great systems on the market. I have developed
one called a MAP: Money Allocation Plan. Presently it is a manual

73

system and is not available on computer. The system operates on one piece of paper (11 x 17) every month. That's all you need. The Money Allocation Plan does not teach you to track every dime you spend! It is a simple plan that is easy to use.

In the few pages that follow, let me share my story with you and teach you how to use the Money Allocation Plan.

## My Story

I did not marry Janet directly out of college. In fact, I purchased a house in Dallas, Texas, as a single and lived there for three years with two roommates who worked in the same office with me. On many days at about five we would meet to decide who would cook the meal that night. The "chosen" person would leave the office, stop by the grocery store, buy the food, and then cook the meal. We lived day by day.

When I married Janet, she moved in, and the guys moved out. One of the first things she checked out was the kitchen. She quickly realized the cupboards were almost bare. Sure, we had salt, pepper, and lemon pepper, but that was the extent of our spices.

"I think we need to go grocery shopping," she immediately said.

"Great!" I agreed. I could picture us holding hands as we walked through the aisles together. I enjoyed being with Janet, no matter what we were doing.

Janet selected a large grocery cart, and we began going up and down every aisle. Eventually the top part of the cart was full and overflowing, and so was the bottom. (I wasn't holding Janet's hand anymore because the grocery cart was so full, it took both of us to push it! Just kidding!)

Finally, we made it to the checkout counter, and the clerk began to ring up the items. The total was almost $200! (I don't think the checkout girl had ever seen a grown man crying as he was writing out the check.) Then I turned to Janet and said something like, "Janet, I buy groceries by the day, not by the year."

Well, she didn't appreciate that very much. So we went home and "discussed" it some more.

## THE TWO SHALL BECOME ONE

Before we were married, Janet and I had a great financial relationship, we decided. She had her checkbook and spent money exactly as she pleased. I had my checkbook and spent money exactly as I pleased. It was an amiable relationship. Then the two checkbooks became one. Our checkbook. Every time either of us wanted to buy something, we felt an obligation to talk to the other person.

Finally, Janet came to me and said, "Ethan, I think we need a budget." (She did not know to use the word *MAP*.) I answered, "I think you are right." That was the beginning of the first Money Allocation Plan (MAP).

## PLANNING YOUR MAP

The first thing we did was to decide how much money we projected to come in that year. Then we asked the question, "Where do we need to allocate it?" After several hours we had determined how we would give, save, and spend our money.

The MAP helps to take the financial stress out of a marriage. If there is money in the clothing allocation, go spend it. No talking, no discussion necessary. If there is no money in the furniture or golfing account, you wait until the money builds back up. There is no need to pout or to scheme or even to talk about it. Period!

Without a MAP some families have to discuss every spending decision. Or if they don't discuss it, they end up fighting over every item purchased. Or even worse, one spouse hides a purchase from the other to avoid a confrontation, and the other spouse hides money in a secret account so it won't all be spent.

A smart money manager has a Money Allocation Plan. I highly recommend it to everyone who is trying to find some freedom in managing his or her money.

## YOUR FINANCIAL MAP:
## THE MONEY ALLOCATION PLAN

I have personally been using and teaching people how to use a Money Allocation Plan since 1982. It is a simple plan anyone can use. There are three quick benefits to this plan:

**It's easy to use!**

All you need is one MAP per month (twelve per year). You don't need anything complex or a notebook full of tabs and paper.

**It provides the big picture!**

The MAP helps you to focus on the big picture, not on the insignificant details. On twelve pieces of paper, you will have your entire financial life documented. You will have a record of all your income and expenses for the year, and you will quickly be able to see where the money came from and where it went.

You will now be able to oversee your finances with a simple and easy-to-use resource.

**You'll waste less money!**

It's a fact, if you live on a MAP, you will waste less money. Why? Because now you have a plan, and you can maximize your resources. The MAP brings freedom, not bondage.

Don't be fooled by three prevalent budget myths:

- Budgets are bondage.
- Budgets take all the fun out of life.
- Budgets are too complex.

**A Sample MAP**

Take a look at the sample MAP on pages 97–100.

Let me begin by explaining the big picture of how the Money Allocation Plan works; then I will move to the specific details. In using a MAP, you determine ahead of time how your money (income) will be allocated into numerous budget categories. Before you begin, understanding the word *allocation* is important in using a MAP.

Think of using a MAP in this way: Picture yourself working in a post office. There are numerous boxes on the wall with little doors on the other side, and your job is to "allocate" the mail into the proper boxes. Some mailboxes have lots of mail while others have little or none. Later on in the day, people come along and take the mail out of the boxes. If you have not put any mail in a particular box, they cannot take anything out of the box.

The MAP is very similar. Every time you receive a paycheck, you take this money and "allocate" it into various money boxes, according to its predetermined address, for example, food or clothing. When you write a check or spend money, you are taking money out of the box. Before you go shopping, you might want to look on your MAP to see how much money (if any) remains in a particular category or box. If the allocation box in your MAP is empty, you cannot spend money in that category. If there is money in that category, it will be fine to spend it. That is why it is there!

Now let's look at the first page of the sample MAP. As you read the following notes, flip back to look at what we are discussing.

**Front Page**

The box on the top of the page is where you record all the income you receive for your family. Examples of things you would record in this income box would be:

- Paychecks
- Bonus check
- Interest income for checking account
- Dividend income
- Gift money
- Hobby income
- Tax refund money
- All the income you ever put into your checking account!

Notice how this section has a place for the date, source, and income account.

**Date**–Always record the date you received the income and deposited it in your checking account.

**Source of Income**–In this space list the source of the income. If you work for ABC Company, that is exactly what you would write here. If you received a dividend check from Jones & Co., you would list "Jones & Co." in this space. Write down the source of all your income!

**Budgeted or Nonbudgeted**–Did you plan, or budget, for this money? Is this money to be used as a part of your regular household budget money? If the answer is yes, it is "budgeted income." Examples of budgeted income usually include your salary and any other sources of income you expect to receive and use for your regular household expenses. If the answer is no, you call it nonbudgeted income. Examples of nonbudgeted income include gift money, bonus checks, and business reimbursements. Put the amount in the proper budgeted or nonbudgeted column.

**Total Deposit**–This column is used for the total dollar amount for each individual deposit made during the current month. Some deposits will have only one check, while other deposits will have two or more checks. If you have only one check to deposit, the total deposit column will be the same as the amount you put in either the budgeted or the nonbudgeted column. If you have several checks, the grand total for budgeted and nonbudgeted will equal the amount in the total deposit column.

Immediately below the income chart at the top of the front page is the allocation work sheet.

**Category**–The first column on this work sheet is where you will list all your budget categories for your family. There is no set list of categories because your list should include categories that your family needs, not what my family needs.

Here are some of the most common budget categories most families will use. Your family will not need to use every category I have listed:

- Allowance: husband
- Allowance: wife
- Auto expenses: gasoline, oil, tires, repairs

- Auto insurance
- Car payment/savings
- Children: allowances, toys, sports
- Clothing: husband
- Clothing: children
- Clothing: wife
- Debt repayment: for all past debts you have incurred
- Food
- Gifts: birthday, anniversary, baby, Christmas
- Giving: local church and other ministries
- Home repair
- Household: furniture, appliances, supplies
- Life insurance
- Medical: insurance, doctor bills, prescriptions
- Miscellaneous
- Mortgage/rent
- Savings, retirement
- Savings, short-term
- Savings, college
- Savings, emergency fund
- School expense
- Social: eating out
- Telephone
- Utilities: gas, electric, water
- Vacations

**Budget $**–This is where you put the amount you are going to allocate for the month into the specific category. This is your planned budget for the month. The sample MAP plans to have $3,200 in income, so the total of all the amounts in this column for all the allocations equals this amount.

By allocating your money this way, this is what you are saying: "I plan to receive $3,200 in income this month, and I plan to allocate/distribute this money into the following twenty-one budget categories."

Determining how much you need to allocate into each category is one of your biggest challenges. The first time you do this will be your most time-consuming. In determining how much you need for each category, consider the following points.

For MAP categories that are fixed amounts, such as mortgage or rent, the process is easy; just fill in the amount you need for the month. For example, if your mortgage payment is $600, this is the amount you must allocate into that category.

Next, you need to deal with expenses that are not monthly but are quarterly, semiannual, or annual expenses. For example, if your car insurance premium of $600 is due once every six months, you will need to allocate $100 each month into an insurance MAP category. In six months, when the premium is due, you will have all the needed money in your MAP insurance category.

If you plan to spend $300 for Christmas, why not allocate $25 each month into a Christmas category during the year? The same would be true for an annual life insurance premium. If the premium is $500, allocate $42 each month into your life insurance category.

Examples of nonmonthly expenses may include auto insurance, life insurance, disability insurance, vacations, and Christmas expenses.

By taking a major expense and allocating funds into your MAP category, or money box, each month, you will take away the stress of major expenses and find that life is a lot easier when you have money in your category to cover this major expense.

You will definitely need to put more thought and planning into how much you will allocate for MAP categories such as food, clothing, savings, and social, but once again you are looking at the financial needs for one month.

The first time you do this may take some time, but for the future months, all the work is done, and you simply use the same amounts each month!

**Deposit Amounts from Chart Above**–Each time you make a deposit, record it in the first available deposit column in the chart.

Our illustration shows a family receiving $1,500 in income on March 1. This amount from the income chart on the top of the page is transferred to the deposit column on the bottom of the page. Your next job is to decide how you want to allocate this income. Notice, in our example, this $1,500 was allocated into the mortgage ($600), debt repayment ($100), short-term savings ($150), utilities ($150), food ($350), and giving ($150) categories. You will do this for each deposit you make in your checking account. The first few months will take more time because the whole process is new. However, over time, if you follow a regular routine for how each paycheck will be distributed in which categories, the process will become much faster and easier. Notice how the total for all the allocations equals the total deposit!

Next let's look at the two inside and back pages of the MAP.

**Inside and Back Pages (pages 98–100)**

The two inside pages and the back page are used for all your different MAP categories, or money boxes. The first thing you notice is that the boxes are all different sizes; different size categories are to be used for different purposes. The larger ones are to be used for categories with frequent use, such as food. I don't know about your family, but we write more checks to the grocery store than anywhere else.

The small ones are to be used for budget categories that usually have one or two entries each month. Examples are categories such as mortgage, insurance, or long-term savings.

Your next job is to "transfer" each allocated amount (from the front page) to the appropriate MAP category on the inside and back pages of the MAP. Notice how the $600 allocated for mortgage was transferred to the mortgage category on the inside page of the MAP; the $600 was put in the + column. This makes $600 available in the mortgage money box. Until now, the box was empty, and you had no money available to use for a mortgage payment! The same transfers are made for the remaining categories: You will transfer $100 into the debt repayment category (or money box), $150 into the short-term savings category, $150 into the utilities category, $350 into the food category, and $150 into the giving category!

Now you have received income, allocated it, and transferred it to the proper categories. Your money boxes, or categories, now have $1,500 more money in them for you to use during the coming days, weeks, and months. Let's look at how those categories and columns work.

**D/# Column**–Notice how each category has a variety of columns. The first column is the "D/#" column. This is to be used for either the date or the check number. I recommend you use dates for "plus transactions" (income allocations) and check numbers for "minus transactions" (expenses) in each category.

**BB**

I might point out that BB on the first line for each category stands for "beginning balance". At the end of each month, you will transfer the ending balance in each category to the BB line of each category.

**+ Column**–Use the plus column when you are allocating money into a budget category. For example, look at the food category. In the D/# column, you see "3–1," representing March 1, and $350 in the plus column. This tells you that on March 1 you allocated $350 into your food category.

**MAP tip**–When using the MAP categories, round your entry to the nearest whole dollar. Notice how this has been done on the sample MAP. Rounding will save you hours every month. You do not need to keep your MAP to the penny! However, be sure to keep your checkbook register to the penny.

**– Column**–Use the minus column when you spend money in this particular category. Look again at the food category. In the D/# column we see 505. We also see $60 in the minus column and $311 in the equals column. This tells us we wrote check number 505 for $60 and we have $311 remaining dollars to be spent for food this month.

If for some reason you wanted to find out what store you wrote the check to and when it was dated, you could go to your checkbook register and look up check number 505.

**= Column**–The first entry in the equals column shows the beginning balance (BB) for the month. For example, in the food category, we had $21 left over in the food category when February ended. Therefore, we simply transfer the ending food balance of $21 to the beginning balance for the food category for March. This column tells you how much money you have remaining in your category. If it has a balance, you have money available to spend. If this column is empty, you do not have any money to spend in this category until you allocate some more money into it.

**Item Column**–Notice how some categories have an additional column labeled "item." These categories are used for expense categories where it would be helpful to have some additional data in the MAP. I recommend you use these for categories such as giving, miscellaneous, medical, savings, insurance, and reimbursement. Study the sample MAP to see how this is done. For example, in the giving category, you can list in the item column who received the gift, or in the reimbursement category you can list what you bought. This information can help you fill out a reimbursement form at a later date. This is done because it might be helpful to have more detailed information for your giving, medical, or insurance expenditure. But most people really do not need detailed information about purchases for food and clothing.

**Credit Cards**–As you can imagine, the credit card category is important. Look at the credit card category in the sample MAP, and let's discuss the first transaction.

On March 17, you filled up your car with gasoline and charged the gas on your MasterCard. When you update the budget at the end of the week, you record this charge and budget the expense in the following way:

You put the date "3/17" in the D/# column of the credit card category. This records the date you actually made the purchase. It is helpful to have the purchase date when your bill arrives in the mail.

Next, you put "gas" or the store name in the item column. This tells you what you purchased and/or from whom.

Then in the "Transfer From" column you put the category you are spending money out of. In our example our purchase was for gas, so it will come out of our car expense category. Think about it; even though this is a credit card purchase, you have still spent money! Money must be immediately taken out of the car expense category and put into your credit card category.

Now look at the last entry in the car expense category. You will find the letters CC in the D/# column. This indicates a credit card transfer. Notice the 20 in the minus column. We are taking $20 out of car expenses and putting $20 into the credit card category. Now we have $50 remaining in our car expense category.

Now your MAP shows that you have less money in your car expenses category to be spent, and you have more money in your credit card category, so when the bill arrives you already have money in your credit card category to pay it! In post office terms, we are simply "forwarding" the money to another address. It was originally allocated to the car expense category; now it is being forwarded to a new address: credit card category.

Next, put the name of the card (MC) in the "Card" column. This will help you when it comes time to pay all the MasterCard charges.

Now, put the charge amount ($20) in the plus column of the credit card category. This might seem strange, putting what you just charged in the plus column, but this is exactly what you need to do. Remember, we just took $20 out of the car expense category and now we are putting it into the credit card category until the bill comes and we need to take it out!

Now the ending balance in the credit card category is $120. In our illustration, $100 was the beginning balance brought forward from last month. In other words, we already had $100 in our credit card money box from charges last month. This money will be used to pay the credit card bill that will arrive this month. When the bill comes, go back to last month's budget and place a check in the paid column beside each entry that is being paid; then write the check to MasterCard.

Find where we wrote check number 536 in the credit card category. Note that this amount ($100) is recorded in the minus column, and the new balance of $135 is recorded in the equals column. The $135 balance in the credit card category represents the total of all outstanding credit card charges we have made this month.

It is best to update your credit card charges weekly to keep your budget categories current. If you did not reflect your credit card charges immediately, it would be easy to overspend because it takes most credit card bills twenty-five to thirty days to arrive in your mailbox. By updating the credit card expenses weekly, you know exactly how much you actually have to spend in each category.

## Balancing and Updating the MAP Weekly

Either Janet or I update our MAP once a week. We sit down with our checkbook, the MAP, a pencil, and a calculator. This is when we record on our MAP all the financial activities that took place in our checkbook during the week.

The updating must take place at least weekly to let you know how you are doing in all your MAP categories. In my opinion, if you update your MAP only once a month, you are simply wasting your time. You are not budgeting but spending a lot of time tracking where all the money went!

That's right, each week you sit down with your checkbook and update the budget categories. Put a check next to each entry in your checkbook, documenting that the expense item has been recorded in the MAP. Next week when you update the budget again, you will know where to begin.

## Balancing the Budget Each Week

Now here is an important aspect of making the MAP work. The total balances of all the MAP categories should equal the balance in your checkbook.

If we added the ending balances of every category in our sample MAP, they would equal $4,464. This should be the same amount in your checkbook. You see, as money goes into your checkbook, you are putting money into all the MAP categories. As you spend money out of your checkbook, you are taking money out of your MAP categories.

**As money goes into your checkbook, MAP total increases.**

**As money goes out of your checkbook, MAP total decreases.**

Let's look once again at our example: If you look at the sample MAP, you will find the following ending balances:

| | |
|---|---:|
| Mortgage | $ 0 |
| Car payment/savings | 2,200 |
| Taxes | 225 |
| Car expenses | 50 |
| Household | 60 |
| Clothing | 60 |
| Children | 60 |
| Gifts | 120 |
| House repair | 110 |
| Allowance (H) | 68 |
| Allowance (W) | 73 |
| Social | 2 |
| Utilities | 94 |
| Food | 6 |
| Miscellaneous | 62 |
| Insurance | 270 |
| Giving | 45 |
| Short-term savings | 450 |
| Credit cards | 255 |
| Debt repayment | 0 |
| Medical | 124 |
| Business reimbursement | 130 |
| Long-term savings | 0 |
| Total for all categories | $4,464 |

**Checkbook Balance = Total of All Map Categories**

When I add them up each week, the grand total should equal the balance in my checkbook. However, due to rounding, you might have a difference of a few dollars plus or minus.

This is what you do to correct this small difference between your checkbook and your MAP. If the MAP total is less than your checkbook balance, add the difference to your miscellaneous category. Look at the miscellaneous category on our sample MAP. Notice the "Item" column says, "Bal. Budget" and the plus column has a 2 in it. This is where I adjusted the MAP to equal the balance in my checkbook.

If the MAP total is *more* than your checkbook, subtract the difference from your miscellaneous category. If the difference is more than $5, you have probably made an error in recording somewhere. The simplest way to find the error is to go back through your checkbook and double-check each transfer of information from your checkbook to the MAP. This is another reason to update your MAP weekly; it's easier to find a mistake when you are reviewing twenty-five entries, compared to one hundred entries.

### A New MAP Each Month

You will use a new MAP each month, transferring all the ending balances from last month's MAP to the BB (beginning balances) column of the current month's MAP.

Another important perspective in using your MAP is how you handle your income when it arrives.

### All Income Goes into the Checkbook

Record 100 percent of your income on your MAP. Do not cash a paycheck and put $100 in your pocket, then deposit the rest in your checking account. Deposit the entire paycheck and then, if needed, write a check for $100 and cash it. By following this procedure, you have established a clear "paper trail" to document your income and expense activities.

### Pay All Expenses Out of the Checkbook

Try to pay for everything by check with the exception of "small personal expenses." These should be paid out of the personal allowance money you carry in your pocket. This is the money you use for lunch, sports, haircuts, and personal items.

Since we are on the topic of personal allowance money, let me explain why it is so important for every MAP to have these categories.

**Personal Allowance Categories**

Personal allowance categories are required for your family to find freedom! I do not recommend you walk around with three-by-five cards recording every penny you spend. You should establish a minimum amount per month for each spouse. In my opinion, this is a nonnegotiable budget item. You must allow some personal money! You should be free to spend for small things without having to record every dollar.

Your personal allowance money is the cash you keep in your wallet. When you need personal allowance money, you should write a check and cash it at the bank. This cashed check is recorded in the minus column of the personal allowance category on the MAP.

Find the "Allowance (H)" category on our sample MAP. Notice that check number 504 was written for $50. This means the husband went to the bank, cashed a check for $50, and put the money in his pocket. This money can now be spent for personal expenses during the week or month.

However, if you do have a large personal allowance expense, it is fine to write a check. This check will then be recorded later in your personal allowance category. But remember, *always* try to use the checks when you spend money for nonpersonal expenses such as groceries, monthly bills, clothing, and gifts.

Now I feel the need to get really personal at this point. From my years of helping people in money management, I must make a few comments to men or women who are tightwads.

**A Personal Note to Tightwads**

I have observed that some spouses like to keep a real "tight" budget. Everyone in the family is instructed to record every penny he or she spends on a three-by-five card to be turned in each day (or some other modification of this plan).

If this is true of you, loosen up! These plans seldom work, especially if you demand that it be done *your* way. Give your spouse freedom! It is not just your money. It's his or her money too! This allowance account is intended to give each spouse freedom to make his or her own choices. Don't fight over how every penny was or will be spent. In my opinion, this is one sure way to take all the fun out of a marriage.

**Spend Based on the MAP Category, Not the Checkbook Balance**

If you are operating on a MAP, your checkbook balance will grow because you are allocating on a monthly basis for Christmas, car insurance premiums, and future things like vacations. *You must not spend based on the checkbook balance but on each individual budget category balance.* Your checkbook balance has been allocated into many different categories. Spend according to what your MAP says you have to spend.

**MAP Account "Paper Transfers"**

You can do budget account transfers any time you like. For example, if I go by the grocery store and do not have the checkbook but spend $20 of my personal allowance money, I can put the grocery store bill in my billfold and, at the end of the week when I update the budget, transfer $20 from the food category to my personal allowance category.

Look at the food and husband's allowance categories on the sample MAPS. You will see $20 was taken out of the food MAP category and $20 was put into the husband's allowance MAP category.

**When a Category Becomes a Minus**

When you run out of money in a category, stop spending money in that category! Next, decide from which positive-balance category you want to transfer funds. If you continually run negative balances in your MAP, you are wasting your time, and the system has lost all its integrity. It is not helping you, and you might as well throw the MAP in the trash can. You must work at keeping all categories in a positive or zero balance. If you keep having a negative balance, you need to increase your monthly allocation for that category and lower the monthly allocation for a category running a positive balance.

**Debt Repayment Category**

If you have outstanding debts you are paying off monthly (not including your home or car), you need to have a debt repayment category on your MAP. For example, this category would be used if you have outstanding credit card debt *when you first begin using the MAP.* You do not pay "old credit card debt" out of the credit card category. Others items that might fall in this category are old school loans, furniture or appliance loans, and medical bills that had not been paid when you started using a MAP. You need to allocate money into your debt repayment category just like you allocate money into the food category. *If you have debt, then debt repayment should be a high priority in any budget!*

Note: All future credit card purchases should go into the credit card category so you can pay each month's bill in full.

**Should I Keep All the Budget Money in a Checking Account?**

The first rule for your checking account should be to find one that pays interest.

Second, as a general rule of thumb, I recommend you keep the equivalent of one month's salary in your checking account. If your checking account balance consistently is more than the equivalent of one month's salary, you should transfer the surplus into a money market account where it will earn more than it does in your checking account. Most money market accounts allow you to write *only* three to five checks per month. However, some allow you to transfer funds between your checking and money market account several times each month.

When you need funds to pay for a large expense such as an annual life insurance premium, Christmas, or semiannual car insurance premium, you simply transfer funds out of your money market account into your checking account. After the funds have been transferred, you write the check out of your checkbook.

By using this plan, you are able to earn additional interest while having the money available for your use.

Note: If you are using a checking account and money market account, the formula to balance the budget is as follows:

Total of all MAP categories =

total of checking account balance + money market account balance

**Investments**

Except for short-term savings and emergency funds, investments are not kept within the MAP system once you write the check and make the investment. For example, if you are saving $150 each month for retirement, these funds remain in the MAP until you write the check. On the back page study the long-term savings category. You will notice a transfer on 3-10 for $1,000, which was taken out and put into an IRA. IRAs and other investments should be accounted for on a personal balance sheet. Savings for college, if kept in a mutual fund, would also be accounted for outside the MAP system. Investment money just "flows through" the MAP; you initially put the funds in the MAP but later remove them from the system once the investment is purchased.

Now, for one of the most important questions: How do I begin my MAP?

**How to Begin Your MAP**

To begin, you will need a blank MAP. See information at the end of this chapter to order a one-year supply of MAPs.

1. On the first page, fill in the MAP categories and the amounts you have decided to budget for each one. It's easiest if you begin at the first of the month so you don't have to determine partial amounts to budget in each category.

2. Fill in all the category headings (food, clothes, giving, etc.) on the inside and back pages of your MAP.

3. Next, allocate your present checkbook balance into your MAP, allocating these funds into the various categories in the budget. You choose where you want to allocate the funds. If you are beginning

with $500 in your checkbook, you might choose to put $250 in savings and $250 in the food category.

4. Now the total of your checkbook balance should equal the total of all your MAP budget categories.

5. Finally, begin using the MAP as you make the deposits and write checks, following the previous instructions.

## How Should People on Flexible Incomes or Commissions Budget?

While speaking at my seminars, I frequently hear, "But I don't receive the same income every month!" Those people who have an inconsistent income or income based on commissions particularly need to budget! Base your MAP on an average month's income. During the months of an income surplus, put away the surplus into a money market account, and during lesser months withdraw the difference from the same account.

For anyone, discipline is the key to budgeting. When your income for the month is high, put aside a portion of the income to supplement the income when it is low. The goal is to obtain a consistent level of lifestyle from month to month. If you have been incorrectly basing your budget on $2,500 in monthly income but only $2,000 is actually coming in, *change your lifestyle!*

Study the following example:

Determine the average monthly income you received during the prior year:

| Jan | $3,000 | Feb | $2,000 | Mar | $2,500 |
|-----|--------|-----|--------|------|--------|
| Apr | 1,000 | May | 1,500 | Jun | 1,700 |
| Jul | 2,700 | Aug | 2,400 | Sept | 4,000 |
| Oct | 2,000 | Nov | 500 | Dec | 2,200 |

The average equals the total income divided by twelve: $2,125 per month. I would recommend that this family budget their giving, saving, and spending on $2,000 every month. Be conservative when you operate on inconsistent income. It is easier to deal with a surplus each month than a shortfall!

The graph below shows why an inconsistent lifestyle can easily lead to *stress and depression* when the actual income drops below the budgeted income. One month you eat steak and lobster, the next month hot dogs and chips.

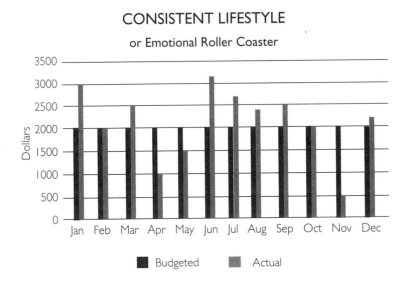

You need to have a money market account to store your surplus income.

**How to Use a Money Market Account and a Checking Account**

When more than $2,000 is earned, be faithful to deposit the excess earnings in a money market account.

When less than $2,000 is earned, determine the shortfall. If you earned only $1,500 this month, the shortfall is $500. Therefore you will need to transfer $500 from the money market account into your checking account. The $1,500 in earnings plus the $500 from the money market account will equal your budgeted need of $2,000.

Study the chart at the bottom of the page and note that when income exceeds $2,000 for the month, we save the excess in a money market account. When the income is less than $2,000, we transfer money out of the money market account and put it into the checking account. First, let me explain what the various columns represent:

**Income Column**–Income received for the current month.

**MM + Column**–This is the amount of money to be deposited in the money market account. Determine this figure by taking the income for the month (i.e., $3,000 in January) and subtracting the planned budget amount ($2,000): $3,000 - $2,000 = $1,000.

**MM – Column**–This amount of money was transferred out of the money market and into the checking account to make up for the income shortfall for the month.

**MM Bal**–The current balance in the money market account each month is shown in this column. This money is available to be transferred into checking when income is less than $2,000 per month.

**Checking Deposit**–The total funds deposited into the checking account each month are shown here. This amount is either 100 percent of the income for the month or a combination of income and the money transferred from the money market. Notice the amount is consistently $2,000 every month.

| Income | | MM + | MM - | MM Bal | Checking Deposit |
|--------|------|--------|--------|--------|------------------|
| Jan | $3,000 | $1,000 | $0 | $1,000 | $2,000 |
| Feb | 2,000 | 0 | 0 | 1,000 | 2,000 |
| Mar | 2,500 | 500 | 0 | 1,500 | 2,000 |
| Apr | 1,000 | 0 | 1,000 | 500 | 2,000 |
| May | 1,500 | 0 | 500 | 0 | 2,000 |
| June | 3,200 | 1,200 | 0 | 1,200 | 2,000 |
| Jul | 2,700 | 700 | 0 | 1,900 | 2,000 |
| Aug | 2,400 | 400 | 0 | 2,300 | 2,000 |
| Sep | 2,500 | 500 | 0 | 2,800 | 2,000 |
| Oct | 2,000 | 0 | 0 | 2,800 | 2,000 |
| Nov | 500 | 0 | 1,500 | 1,300 | 2,000 |
| Dec | 2,200 | 200 | 0 | 1,500 | 2,000 |

**What If I Don't Have a Money Market Account?**

If you don't have a money market account to fall back on, you have only one option: allocate exactly what came in! Ask yourself, based on the money I do have, how do I want to allocate it? *Don't use debt to live beyond your means!*

If this is your situation for more than three months, lower your planned budget allocations until the circumstances change! Be faithful to be a good steward over the resources God has entrusted to you at this time. It is better to lower your standard of living and be realistic than to keep living at a level of income you are not presently earning. If and when your income increases, then you will have the freedom to raise your budget allocations.

**Purpose of MAP**

1. *Allow you to be generous in your giving.* I believe that everyone desires to be a generous giver and that using a MAP will help this to become a reality.

2. *Allow you to be consistent in your saving.* Setting aside a small portion of your income each month is the key to keeping you out of debt and meeting the future needs of your family.

3. *Allow you to find freedom in your spending.* Just imagine–no more long hours of discussing whether you have enough to buy more clothes or a computer. If the money has been allocated, go spend it! If you have no money available in your MAP category, you have no need to discuss it.

Be patient as you begin using the MAP system. Give it time to work.

**More Fun Fewer Fights**

Your MAP will enable you to have more fun and less fighting. Now how does that sound?

## How to Order Your MAPs

If you are interested in learning how you can order a one-year supply of the Money Allocation Plan (8 1/2 X 11) and an instructional cassette tape, just write me at the following address:

**Foundations for Living**
**P.O. Box 15356**
**Hattiesburg, MS 39404**

**Or you can visit my Web site at www.foundationsforliving.org.**

## Scripture to Ponder

Read Proverbs 27:23–27.

## Action Step

Pull out your calendar and block out at least three evenings (or one full day) to work on chapters 6, 7, and 8. Without a plan you will not be able to accomplish your goal!

## Money Allocation Plan

| Date | Source of Income | Budgeted | Non-Budgeted | Total Deposit |
|------|-----------------|----------|--------------|---------------|
| 3-1 | ABC Company | 1,500 | | 1,500 |
| 3-15 | ABC Company | 1,700 | | 1,700 |
| | | | | |
| | | | | |
| | | | | |
| | | | | |
| | | | | |
| | | | | |
| | | | | |
| | Totals for Month | $3,200 | $ | $3,200 |

### Allocation Worksheet

| MAP Category | Budget $ | Deposit Amounts from Income Chart Above | | | | | | | | |
|--------------|----------|---------|---------|----|----|----|----|----|----|----|
| | $3,200 | $1,500 | $1,700 | $ | $ | $ | $ | $ | $ | $ |
| Mortgage | 600 | 600 | | | | | | | | |
| Insurance | 120 | | 120 | | | | | | | |
| Taxes | 75 | | 75 | | | | | | | |
| Debt Repayment | 100 | 100 | | | | | | | | |
| Car Pay/Savings | 200 | | 200 | | | | | | | |
| Car Expenses | 170 | | 170 | | | | | | | |
| S. Term Savings | 150 | 150 | | | | | | | | |
| L. Term Savings | 150 | | 150 | | | | | | | |
| Utilities | 150 | 150 | | | | | | | | |
| Home Repair | 75 | | 75 | | | | | | | |
| Food | 350 | 350 | | | | | | | | |
| Children | 50 | | 50 | | | | | | | |
| Giving | 320 | 150 | 170 | | | | | | | |
| Social | 50 | | 50 | | | | | | | |
| Clothing | 130 | | 130 | | | | | | | |
| Medical | 100 | | 100 | | | | | | | |
| Household | 50 | | 50 | | | | | | | |
| Gifts | 60 | | 60 | | | | | | | |
| Allowance (H) | 100 | | 100 | | | | | | | |
| Allowance (W) | 100 | | 100 | | | | | | | |
| Misc. | 100 | | 100 | | | | | | | |

| Mortgage | | | | Car Pay/Savings | | | | Taxes | | | | | | | |
|---|---|---|---|---|---|---|---|---|---|---|---|---|---|---|---|
| D/# | + | − | = | D/# | + | − | = | D/# | + | − | = | D/# | + | − | = |
| BB | | | 0 | BB | | | 2000 | BB | | | 150 | BB | | | |
| 3-1 | 600 | | 600 | 3-15 | 200 | | 2200 | 3-15 | 75 | | 225 | | | | |
| 501 | | 600 | 0 | | | | | | | | | | | | |

| Car Expenses | | | | Household | | | | Clothing | | | | Children | | | |
|---|---|---|---|---|---|---|---|---|---|---|---|---|---|---|---|
| D/# | + | − | = | D/# | + | − | = | D/# | + | − | = | D/# | + | − | = |
| BB | | | 140 | BB | | | 40 | BB | | | 100 | BB | | | 60 |
| 3-15 | 170 | | 310 | 508 | | 12 | 28 | 3-15 | 130 | | 230 | 509 | | 25 | 35 |
| 512 | | 80 | 230 | 3-15 | 50 | | 78 | 514 | | 80 | 150 | 3-15 | 50 | | 85 |
| 513 | | 160 | 70 | 529 | | 18 | 60 | CC | | 90 | 60 | 538 | | 25 | 60 |
| CC | | 20 | 50 | | | | | | | | | | | | |

| Gifts | | | | House Repair | | | | | | | | | | | |
|---|---|---|---|---|---|---|---|---|---|---|---|---|---|---|---|
| D/# | + | − | = | D/# | + | − | = | D/# | + | − | = | D/# | + | − | = |
| BB | | | 80 | BB | | | 80 | BB | | | | BB | | | |
| 3-15 | 60 | | 140 | 3-15 | 75 | | 155 | | | | | | | | |
| 527 | | 20 | 120 | 527 | | 45 | 110 | | | | | | | | |

| Allowance H | | | | Allowance W | | | | Social | | | | Utilities | | | |
|---|---|---|---|---|---|---|---|---|---|---|---|---|---|---|---|
| D/# | + | − | = | D/# | + | − | = | D/# | + | − | = | D/# | + | − | = |
| BB | | | 68 | BB | | | 93 | BB | | | 37 | BB | | | 92 |
| 504 | | 50 | 18 | 507 | | 50 | 43 | 503 | | 10 | 27 | 3-1 | 150 | | 242 |
| 3-15 | 100 | | 118 | 3-1 | 110 | | 143 | 3-15 | 50 | | 77 | 516 | | 19 | 223 |
| 528 | | 20 | 98 | 520 | | 50 | 93 | 519 | | 50 | 27 | 517 | | 82 | 141 |
| 534 | | 50 | 48 | 537 | | 20 | 73 | CC | | 25 | 2 | 518 | | 47 | 94 |
| Food | 20 | | 68 | | | | | | | | | | | | |

## Food

| D/# | + | − | = |
|---|---|---|---|
| BB | | | 21 |
| 3-1 | 350 | | 371 |
| 505 | | 60 | 311 |
| 510 | | 19 | 292 |
| 511 | | 37 | 255 |
| 515 | | 97 | 158 |
| 522 | | 53 | 105 |
| 526 | | 60 | 45 |
| 532 | | 19 | 26 |
| A(H) | | 20 | 6 |

## Misc.

| D/# | Item | + | − | = |
|---|---|---|---|---|
| BB | | | | 5 |
| 3-15 | | 100 | | 105 |
| 523 | Cleaners | | 15 | 90 |
| 531 | Cash | | 20 | 70 |
| 540 | Postage | | 10 | 60 |
| | Bal. Budget | 2 | | 62 |

## Insurance

| D/# | Item | + | − | = |
|---|---|---|---|---|
| BB | | | | 240 |
| 3-15 | | | 120 | 360 |
| 541 | Life | | 90 | 270 |

## Giving

| D/# | Item | + | − | = |
|---|---|---|---|---|
| BB | | | | 0 |
| 3-1 | | | 150 | 150 |
| 502 | Church | | 75 | 75 |
| 3-15 | | | 170 | 245 |
| 521 | Church | | 75 | 170 |
| 530 | ABC Min. | | 50 | 120 |
| 535 | Church | | 75 | 45 |

## Short Term Saving

| D/# | + | − | = | D/# | + | − | = | D/# | + | − | = |
|---|---|---|---|---|---|---|---|---|---|---|---|
| BB | | | 300 | BB | | | | BB | | | |
| 3-1 | 150 | | 450 | | | | | | | | |

## Credit Cards

| D/# | Item | Transfer From | Card | PD | + | − | = |
|---|---|---|---|---|---|---|---|
| BB | | | | | | | 100 |
| 3-17 | Gas | Car Expense | MC | | 20 | | 120 |
| 3-19 | Mr. Steak | Social | MC | | 25 | | 145 |
| 3-24 | Fashion Tree | Clothing | MC | | 90 | | 235 |
| 536 | Payment for Last Month | | MC | | | 100 | 135 |
| 3-26 | Hotel-Boston | Business Reimb. | Visa | | 120 | | 255 |

## Long Term Savings

| D/# | + | − | = | D/# | + | − | = | D/# | Item | + | − | = |
|-----|---|---|---|-----|---|---|---|-----|------|---|---|---|
| BB | | | | BB | | | | BB | | | | 850 |
| | | | | | | | | 3-1 | | 150 | | 1000 |
| | | | | | | | | 3-10 | Transfer to IRA | | 1000 | 0 |
| | | | | | | | | | | | | |

## Debt Repay

| D/# | + | − | = | D/# | + | − | = | D/# | Item | + | − | = |
|-----|---|---|---|-----|---|---|---|-----|------|---|---|---|
| BB | | | | BB | | | | BB | | | | 0 |
| | | | | | | | | 3-1 | | 100 | | 100 |
| | | | | | | | | 506 | School Loan | | 50 | 50 |
| | | | | | | | | 525 | Visa | | 50 | 0 |
| | | | | | | | | | | | | |
| | | | | | | | | | | | | |
| | | | | | | | | | | | | |
| | | | | | | | | | | | | |
| | | | | | | | | | | | | |

## Medical

| D/# | + | − | = | D/# | + | − | = | D/# | Item | + | − | = |
|-----|---|---|---|-----|---|---|---|-----|------|---|---|---|
| BB | | | | BB | | | | BB | | | | 94 |
| | | | | | | | | 3-15 | | 100 | | 194 |
| | | | | | | | | 524 | Mary | | 35 | 159 |
| | | | | | | | | 533 | John | | 35 | 124 |
| | | | | | | | | | | | | |
| | | | | | | | | | | | | |

## Business Reimbursement

| D/# | + | − | = | D/# | + | − | = | D/# | Item | + | − | = |
|-----|---|---|---|-----|---|---|---|-----|------|---|---|---|
| BB | | | | BB | | | | BB | | | | 250 |
| | | | | | | | | CC | Hotel-Boston | | 120 | 130 |
| | | | | | | | | | | | | |
| | | | | | | | | | | | | |
| | | | | | | | | | | | | |
| | | | | | | | | | | | | |
| | | | | | | | | | | | | |
| | | | | | | | | | | | | |
| | | | | | | | | | | | | |
| | | | | | | | | | | | | |

## CHAPTER 9

# Some Costly Lures in Life

### MARY

*Instead of saying, 'God, please help me stay home,' it was easier to fix with a credit card.*

When our boys were little, they would say, "Just write a check," when told that we did not have the money to buy something. I remember thinking how funny their response was. They did not realize that good ole mom and dad need to have money in the bank before writing that check!

But today we can often write checks without the money really being in the bank! Jim and I are inundated with offers for credit cards. And often we receive beautiful checks in the mail that almost beg to be used. Recently a very attractive envelope arrived that had a picture of three men fishing in a flat-bottom boat on a calm lake. From the golden hues on the paper, it looked to be just about dawn. The caption on the envelope says in bold letters, "Don't let this one get away!" The back of the envelope reads, "Cast Your Eyes Inside!"

Tempting? You bet!

I'm reminded of Genesis 3:1–7:

> Now the serpent was more crafty than any of the wild animals the LORD God had made. He said to the woman, "Did God really say, 'You must not eat from any tree in the garden'?"
>
> The woman said to the serpent, "We may eat fruit from the trees in the garden, but God did say, 'You must not eat

101

fruit from the tree that is in the middle of the garden, and
you must not touch it, or you will die.'"

"You will not surely die," the serpent said to the woman.
"For God knows that when you eat of it your eyes will be
opened, and you will be like God, knowing good and evil."

When the woman saw that the fruit of the tree was good
for food and pleasing to the eye, and also desirable for
gaining wisdom, she took some and ate it. She also gave
some to her husband, who was with her, and he ate it. Then
the eyes of both of them were opened, and they realized that
they were naked; so they sewed fig leaves together and
made coverings for themselves.

In a way Satan was saying: "Don't let this delicious piece of fruit
get away! Cast your eyes on this big, red beauty!"

We are bombarded today with slick advertising campaigns that
paint pictures that just aren't what they seem to be. Barbara Hoffman,
a jewelry salesman, said: "It's so easy to get swept up by their wonderful offers. It's so easy to spend, and they make it seem so easy to
pay."[1]

I read in our local newspaper: "At the rate credit card issuers are
pushing up fees, Americans could soon pay more in credit card
charges than they spend to insure their homes. Credit card users
spent a record $18.9 billion last year in fees for such offenses as pay-
ing bills late or exceeding a credit limit. An industry research company has found total spending for homeowners' insurance was about
$25 billion."[2]

Mom, something is wrong! How could we get ourselves into a situation where we pay more in credit card fees than we do to insure
our homes? Too many of us have not let the lure of credit get away!

Who can we turn to for advice? Surely pastors and missionaries
have it all together when it comes to credit!

Well, the older I get, the more I realize that no one has it all
together. But we can sure learn from one another along this journey
called life. Pastor Doug Gils and his wife, Kristi, would like you to

learn from their mistakes. (The names of Pastor Doug Gils and his wife Kristi have been changed.)

Kristi said that when she was a little girl, "I just wanted to be a mom, although I kicked around the idea of being a fireman. I knew I wanted to go to college and get an education. I was like a lot of other children and did not put a lot of thought into what I would be doing."

Kristi had graduated from college and was working when she first met Doug in the singles group at church. They had no premarital counseling other than a book that Doug's mother gave them. Shortly after their wedding Doug began his studies at seminary. Initially he worked part-time while Kristi worked full-time at a bank.

It is hard to believe that almost fifteen years have passed since Doug began seminary. He is now in his second pastorate, and he and Kristi even served for over three years on the mission field. Yet today Kristi is not a stay-at-home mom as she planned. What happened?

Kristi explained why she went back to work:

> We made some poor financial decisions. Basically it was a debt issue. There was a financial challenge that we had not prepared for ahead of time. I think if we had planned ahead for my being off work, then it would have been better. Some bills had to be paid.
>
> God takes our mistakes and makes them something educational and beautiful. He has provided this job that I have now. The income it provides more than covers our debt payments plus some, so we can eventually get out of debt again, and that is why I am there.

Her advice to you is: "Plan ahead for as many financial responsibilities (bills you have and know have to be paid even if you are not working). There is no way to get around paying them. There will always be some that you do not see. Plan in great detail.

"The credit card can look so attractive. Mentally you just are not aware of the consequences. You are looking at a solution–now.

"Instead of saying, 'God, please help me stay at home,' it was easier to fix with a credit card."

The Gils' three children go to their church's school. And since they now live in the church parsonage, they feel good knowing that Doug is nearby should the children need him. And yet this is not the picture of home that Doug and Kristi had imagined when they married. Kristi's heart is at home, and she would really like to be at home with her family.

Kristi's story is very different from Susan's. When Susan was seventeen years old, you would have chosen her as one of the least likely candidates to be a godly example in her community. And yet that is exactly what Susan is today. (The name of Susan has been changed.)

As a seventeen-year-old, Susan was not only a high-school dropout but also an unwed mother. She had come from an abusive background and had spent years in the foster care system. Her future looked bleak.

Susan eventually married her high-school sweetheart and became a Christian. Despite her past she was determined to make something of herself. She went back to school and worked hard to receive her GED–graduating, I might add, in the top of her class. And her education did not stop with a high-school diploma. While working part-time, she went to nursing school. Her husband and four young children were rightfully proud of her when she received her nursing certification.

Despite this, Susan's heart began to pull her toward home shortly after she began working in a medical clinic. She had invested so much time and energy into becoming a nurse, yet she and her husband mutually decided that she would return home to care for the children. They moved to the country, enrolled their school-age children in public school, and cut every expense that they could. Because they did not have a lot of debt, they were able to scale back expenses and do what they felt was God's will for their family.

Other than substituting occasionally at school, Susan is home with her kids. When asked if her decision to hang up her stethoscope was worth it, she said, "Being at home with my kids is a bigger job [than being a nurse] and will make a bigger difference in the long run. The kids know I am here when they get home. We are closer, and I talk to them, and I have the time. We are not rushed anymore. It was worth it!"

Both Kristi and Susan have hearts that are "at home"–hearts that are committed to God, their husbands, and children. But why is Susan home while Kristi is still working outside the home? Let's look at Ethan's Five-Step Plan and see if we can determine the reasons. I think number 3 tells why–debt obligations.

Strange as it may seem, Kristi's problems remind me of an aching leg. Let me explain. A couple of months ago I went to the doctor because my leg hurt, so much so that it would even wake me up during the night. He prescribed some medicine and told me to alternate ice and heat on the painful area. I had no problem taking the medicine, and applying the heat was fine–after all, it was warm and felt good to my leg. But the ice, that was a different matter. I tend to be cold natured and was determined not to put ice on my leg.

Weeks went by, my leg was better but still hurt. I told my husband, Jim, that I thought I should return to the doctor and maybe he could give me a shot to make the pain go away. You see, I wanted a quick and easy solution! But Jim said that first I should do exactly what the doctor told me to do. So, much to my dislike, I finally put the ice on my leg. It was so cold! Initially it did not feel good, but it worked, and the pain has gone away.

I now wish I had followed the doctor's entire advice earlier. I had to ask myself, *Why didn't I do what the doctor told me to do in the first place? Why did I choose pain over relief?* The answer is easy: bottom line, I didn't want to do what he said. I thought that I had a better plan, even though I've never gone to medical school. I would do part of what he suggested, but not everything.

I think life (and our finances) can be a lot like this story. We may go to God's Word for expert advice but decide that we don't need to follow it exactly.

The Lord tells us in Luke 14:28 (NASB), "For which one of you, when he wants to build a tower, does not first sit down and calculate the cost, to see if he has enough to complete it?" Too often we do not count the cost and find ourselves in debt. And too often we don't know exactly what to do about it. Too often, after not counting the cost, we complain about our situations.

We are told in Matthew 6:24, "No one can serve two masters. Either he will hate the one and love the other, or he will be devoted to the one and despise the other. You cannot serve both God and Money." I sure want the Lord to be my Master in all that I possess. After all, he owns it all, and we are actually only stewards of his possessions.

We have only to look around and see that choosing God's ways concerning finances will often make us swim against the tide. A *Christian Financial Concepts* online newsletter stated: "In recent years a lot of attention has been focused on the debt of the U.S. government, which now totals $5.6 trillion. There is even a U.S. National Debt Clock on the Internet that monitors federal indebtedness. But many Americans might be shocked if they took time to learn the indebtedness of their city governments. City debts may total in the billions, as indicated by a 1994 report prepared by the Census Bureau."[3]

The article went on to list the amount of debt for particular cities. A few included Los Angeles, $8.4 billion; Chicago, $6.9 billion; and Washington, D.C., $4.1 billion. We know the problem. We buy things when we can't really afford them and then presume on the future. And often we do not want the real answer–just as I did not want to put cold compresses on my leg.

I am reminded of the time when the apostles were being questioned before the high priest for teaching in Jerusalem. Their response to these accusations is recorded in Acts 5:29: "Peter and the other apostles replied: 'We must obey God rather then men!'"

It's amazing to me how we unknowingly choose our masters. I recall times when Jim and I have bought something on credit, presuming on the future. I think of Kristi's words: "There was a financial challenge that we had not prepared for ahead of time. I think if we had planned ahead for my being off work, then I think it would have been better. There were some bills that had to be paid."

And then I see a young woman who knew firsthand what a family should not be–and because of some financial choices and tough decisions, she was able to return home to those she loved.

There's a lot of truth in this saying: "Experience is the hardest kind of teacher. It gives you the test first and the lesson afterward."

So, Mom, when you hear a little voice inside tempting you to go into debt because you think you just can't "let this one get away," think about what it will really cost–if not today, then tomorrow.

**Scriptures to Ponder**

"The earth is the LORD's, and everything in it, the world, and all who live in it" (Ps. 24:1).

"I am God, your God, . . . for every animal of the forest is mine, and the cattle on a thousand hills" (Ps. 50:7–10).

"Keep your lives free from the love of money and be content with what you have, because God has said, 'Never will I leave you; never will I forsake you.' So we say with confidence, 'The Lord is my helper; I will not be afraid'" (Heb. 13:5–6).

**Action Steps**

In the chapter, Kristi said, "Instead of saying, 'God, please help me stay home,' it was easier to fix with a credit card." List a specific time(s) when you were guilty of fixing a situation with debt rather than trusting God. After spending time in prayer with your spouse, list several ways that you can avoid doing this in the future.

CHAPTER 10

# Listening to Moms

ETHAN

> "Most of our wives are planners and meticulous budgeters.
> Most of us will tell you that our wives are a lot more conservative
> with money than we are."
>
> –Thomas Stanley and William Danko, *The Millionaire Next Door*

One of the greatest blessings in writing this book has been my interaction with moms who stay at home full-time or those seriously praying about it. Just by talking with these moms, I have developed such a wealth of information. I personally knew all of these moms, but I have developed a deeper appreciation for each of them as they opened their hearts and shared with me about being a mom. They come from all walks of life and live all over the nation.

As you prepare to become a stay-at-home mom, let me encourage you to listen to the words of wisdom from these stay-at-home moms and let them motivate and inspire you to accomplish your goal! Open your heart and listen to these moms who deeply love God, their family, and especially love their "job."

## Aaryanne Preusch from Hattiesburg, Mississippi

Rick and I had planned from the beginning that I would stay at home with our children. In order to know what is really going on in the lives of my children, I believe I have to spend time with them. My kids just love me being at home. Financially, I look at things realistically. There will always be people who have more and people who don't have as much. I am content with where I am. Let me encourage you to focus your trust on the Lord for him to provide for your family. You really have to deal with the contentment issue–where you place your value and where you get your significance. For me, it's being a mom.

## Barbara Culwell from Austin, Texas

I am at home because I feel like this is a critical time in our family in helping to shape the values of our children. I want to be at home and be available to them every day. Now that they are in school and gone a lot during the day, I have the ability to help keep the house more organized and prepare for our family meals. I have found the more prepared I am as a mom, the less stress we have in our home during the day.

As I try to take time to develop my walk with the Lord, I am in a better position to help my children with the different things they are dealing with during the day. Hopefully, my spiritual life will affect their lives.

The role of a mother is to be a servant, and many times this means you have to deny your own desires. As a mom, you have to do this daily! As moms we need to remember that many of the intangible things we do at home will have lasting value. Remember you should build relationships with other moms. It is important to have other moms just to talk to during the day.

## Dawna Debter from Richardson, Texas

I feel such a high calling to be a mom. Not only am I a caregiver for my children, but it is a role that I take seriously: to be their trainer, teacher, and model who sets the whole atmosphere for the home. Deuteronomy 6:7 says to teach these things to your children. So much teaching can be done in the security of the home, and if I am working or even a stay-at-home mom who is gone all the time, I am not able to focus and to develop and train my children in godliness and righteousness.

My role is to bring order and peace to the home. My role is to make our home the sanctuary or haven for my family when my husband returns home from work and my children return home from school. I believe that creating this environment requires someone to be in the home full time.

My job is to create an environment where my children feel secure and good just about being at home. My advice to any mom leaving the workplace would be for them to develop a sense of calling by spending time in God's Word. By just doing a study of parenting principles from the Book of Proverbs alone, one can glean the vital importance of their influence over their children for eternity. Being a mom at home doesn't get the pats on the back they might be accustomed to receiving in the marketplace. Therefore, you have got to have an anchor that holds you in the dark times, in the silent times, in the lonely times, and in the difficult times. Be in the Word, seek encouragement from like-minded moms, and ask God to equip and encourage you for the journey.

## Donna Scott from South Bend, Indiana

My understanding of being a stay-at-home mom has developed over the years. When Jonathan was first born, I had always heard that it was a good thing to stay at home and I was going on the word of others. Now, five years later, I see the benefits more. I am able to give my children a secure home every day. I am able to teach my children throughout the day godly character and moral convictions. I don't think I could do that as well if I worked outside the home.

I really see that the early years are essential. This is not just textbook information but personal experience for me. I feel like my husband gets the benefits of my being at home; he gets the benefits of an organized home. My convictions of modeling a godly life to my children have become stronger over the years.

My advice to any mom leaving the workplace is to get into a mom's group and meet other moms. Financially, staying at home may be a costly move, but I think that if you have a real understanding of why you want to be at home, you can and will make it work.

The thing that is really important to me is the ability to pour moral and biblical thinking into my child. To me that is everything. That opportunity is worth sacrificing most anything, because that is what God has called me to do. I feel like it is such an honor to be a stay-at-home mom.

## Julie Nutter from Richardson, Texas

I had a deep desire to be with my children once I had them. We decided we would try me staying at home and just see if we could live on Mike's salary. Even in our step of faith, we did not realize what a giant step of faith it really was down the road. We were also willing to do without some things if that was necessary as long as we could provide a home, have food to eat, heat, air-conditioning, and things like that.

Because I am at home, I think our children have a greater sense of family. Being at home and being able to participate in my children's activities has been beneficial for them in their development. When I left the workplace, I went through a period of having some lower self-esteem. When we would be out at social events with Mike's clients and coworkers I would be asked, "Well, what do you do?" I'd respond, "I'm just a mom."

There is no higher investment than in the lives of your children because it is an investment that will last forever. If you are a stay-at-home mom, remember the principle of sowing and reaping. Many times you do not immediately reap of what you are sowing, but down the road you will have a wonderful harvest of your work. It amazes us to look back and to see how the Lord has blessed us. We never dreamed we would be where we are today. The Lord has been so faithful and has continued to bless us over the years.

Being able to stay at home with my children has been such a wonderful blessing. I don't know where Mike heard it, or if it was original with him, but when the girls were small, he used to say, "The days are long, but the years are short." Whenever I write a card to someone who has had a new baby, I always include that saying, "The days are long, but the years are short." I don't want to look back and wish that I would have had those years at home.

## Kay Chastain from Allen, Texas

One of the benefits of my staying at home is that I am able to interact with my children all day. Obviously, financially, there are going to be some sacrifices for any mom to stay at home. However, being able to stay at home with your children is worth any sacrifice. Some days I think, *Well, I have done three loads of laundry and unloaded the dishwasher, but I have been able to instill within my children spiritual values.*

As a mom, I have to focus on why I am doing this. I have to remember, I will not be able to see all the benefits until later in life. Sometimes I feel unappreciated, but I just have to refocus and realize that this is a long-term commitment.

## Kay Ficken from Hattiesburg, Mississippi

My home is my number one priority. Just the other night I was lying in bed thinking what an awesome job I have. I am the "thermostat" of my home. When I have not had my time with God and am not living in the Spirit, I can explode, and the whole house goes haywire. Or, if I am where I spiritually need to be with the Lord, then my house is calm and at peace.

I also think it is so important for my house to be neat and orderly and for our family to have supper together. Being at home helps me to accomplish that. It also helps to bring our family together; we just do a lot together. I don't drive the newest car in town, but God has me where he wants me to be, and I need to be content with what I have.

Financially, a budget has really helped us. On a scale of 1 to 10, the need for us to operate on a budget is definitely a 10! I have to be able to say, "God, you are in control here." God wants me here, and I am so content with being at home, and I have no desire to do anything else.

## Kimberly Moeller from Salt Lake City, Utah

I am a stay-at-home mom primarily because we believe that children are gifts from God and that they are a blessing. My husband and I feel like we are stewards of them, and they will be under our care only a certain number of years when we can truly influence them. We want to make the most of that time and teach them about the Lord. My being at home with them enables me to help train them in obedience, in loving God, and basically to train their hearts. I believe if you are home when they are little that is such a key time to shape their hearts.

You can always step back into the workplace; the work, the degrees, the positions are always there, but the children will be gone. I don't want somebody else giving our children their values. My advice to someone leaving the workplace and coming home would be to remember that this is a season of life, and it won't always be this way. You need a long-term, big-picture perspective of why you are doing what you are doing. In the workplace, the reward is always so immediate–the raise or the praise from the boss–but you don't get that at home.

Being a mom is more of a marathon than a sprint. I don't think that a lot of moms really know the power they have in their home. It's like you are the CEO of your home. You are making financial decisions, educational decisions, and decisions about how your employees (children) are going to be trained. Remember that as you are training your children, God will be changing you as well, so allow him to make you the mom he really wants you to be. Financially, believe that when God provides the sheep, he will provide the pasture. If you are struggling financially, get all of your debts paid off and begin to live within your means. I think the mom needs to see what she does as a "real job." It is not just "staying at home," but it means she needs a plan for the day, a plan for the week, and a plan for the month regarding what she's teaching her children; otherwise the days just go by. I want to be there to teach my children to obey me and my husband so that when they are on their own, they will know how to obey God; and that is really the reason for me to stay at home!

### Laura Messina from Orlando, Flordia

My husband and I decided early on that if the Lord should bless us with children, then I, as a Christian mom, would stay at home. I honestly believe that this whole notion or concept of quality time is garbage. I think it is guilt-ridden time. They are thinking, *I feel guilty because I haven't spent any time with my children. Therefore on the weekends I am going to take them to the movies and do some fabulous, expensive thing.*

I think in order to raise a God-honoring young lady or gentleman, the child needs consistently to be in the presence of God-honoring parents. Our children need to be around me a lot so I can explain to them what the Bible says about Christ and his ways. Our children need to see us helping others and being generous with the resources God has given to us. They can't see that unless they are with us.

I worked at my children's school for two years. We noticed that as a family, when I worked, the stress was not worth the extra dollars coming in. My working translated into too much stress in the house. We agreed as a family (husband, wife, and children) that we wanted mom to come home.

If you are considering coming home, I would advise you first to pray, and second, be sure that the whole family buys into the plan. That way, when you are at home and having to do without some material things or eating out less, it's OK, because everybody bought into the plan.

I believe one of the biggest contributions that a stay-at-home mom can make to the family is the whole atmosphere of the home. In our house, as goes mom, so goes the family. If mom is all stressed out and short-tempered, it seems as if everybody else is at each others' throat also. But if everybody else comes home and I am calm, the entire house is calm.

Being at home has been a good decision for our family, and none of us would vote for me to go back to work. My biggest advice to a young couple starting out would be to try to live on one income when you first get married so you will have the freedom to stay at home with the kids in the future. Because if you need both incomes to pay the mortgage, your options are limited in the future.

**Mary Woodruff from Melissa, Texas**

One of the main reasons I am a stay-home mom is that I disagree with the philosophy that women can "do it all." I understand that some women don't have a choice, but I think that if you choose to work outside the home, something has to give. Usually what is going to give is your family because the best hours of your day are given to the job, and when you come home, you are tired, and so the kids and the family suffer.

But even as a stay-at-home mom, I have to guard my outside commitments for the same reason. If I get too committed doing all those "good" things, the family suffers. If I am too exhausted, I cannot run the home in the manner that Jon and I desire.

Because I grew up with a mom who stayed at home, I reaped a lot of benefits. My mom was extremely involved in what we did and made it possible for us to do a lot of things. Jon and I made a choice to be parents, and part of that choice is for somebody to run the home and raise the children.

Being a mom is a job, and it is an important job. It is a job that has a lot of fulfilling moments. When I had four children at home that were kindergarten age and under, other moms would tell me, "Mary, it really does go by quickly." I would laugh inside and think, *I will be doing this forever.* They were right; the years have gone by quickly.

Even as a stay-at-home mom, I look back with some regrets. I look back at things that I allowed to distract me. You need to try to forget what the world is telling you–that a job would give you satisfaction and is more important than being a mom.

When my kids were little, I had a little bit of the mind-set, "Go ahead and grow up, so I can get back to that stuff I was trained to do in college." Now I just grieve that I had that mind-set and it has taken me several years for the Lord to teach me, "This is your job, and the other stuff is not what I have called you to do."

Who is really going to remember fifty years from now that I wrote a magazine article? What matters is whether you raised godly children and children of character who then go on to raise their own. That is what is going to matter. As my walk with the Lord grows and matures, so does my attitude about being a mother.

## Sheri McGill from Orlando, Florida

I have to focus more on what is really important and how to keep things simple because I do not know what each day or week is going to hold. As I have kept things simple, my roots have gone really deep with the Lord. Sometimes I feel like I am on the front seat of a roller coaster. It is an exciting adventure because sometimes it is fast and sometimes it is slow. In the slow process God nudges me and lets me know that I am of value to him and that I don't need to get my value from the world.

The neat thing about it is that it just goes so against the grain of what the world is saying. Sometimes I turn on *Good Morning America*, and I think, *Oh, look at the life they lead and the clothes they get to wear.* But you really don't know what is going on in their hearts and in their family or in their marriage. They look good, but I would give up all they have because I know that the lasting thing is the relationship you have with the Lord and how that filters down to your family.

I am constantly talking to my children about ways that I feel blessed to be at home. If anyone is considering leaving the workplace, they need to be honest with the Lord and say, "Lord, I am willing to do whatever you want me to do." Then watch and see what he does. Even though it is a leap of faith, it is exciting! My faith has grown tremendously when I do what he has called me to do.

By being a stay-at-home mom, I have the freedom "instantly" to do whatever God might call me to do for myself, my husband, and my family. I am called to work and minister here in the home, and it is so freeing!

Finally, let me share with you what my wife, Janet, said about being a stay-at-home mom:

My strongest conviction for being a stay-at-home mom comes from the fact that when I was growing up I had a working mother. Practically speaking, she just wasn't there all day long. I always wanted my children to have the stability and security of knowing I was there if they needed something. I wanted them to know how much they were loved and that being a mom was the most important job I could possibly have. In the early years (one to twelve) you are the one in control of everything that influences them: TV, radio, friends, places, books, church, and adults. You provide the environment, the learning, the atmosphere that teaches them about values, priorities, and meaning in life.

Their lives are in your hands. The values I want for my children are too important to delegate to someone else. Parents are the primary role models and example. Don't be afraid to face the financial aspect of doing without material things. Yes, it is difficult to sacrifice and struggle to make ends meet. But God will provide in so many incredible ways that will surprise you, delight you, and bless your whole family. God is true to his Word, and he will provide.

Let me conclude this chapter by sharing with you how one mom processed the decision to move from teaching school to staying at home full-time. When I was interviewing Debbie Kennedy, she asked me, "Have you talked with Lesa Gibson?" I responded that I had not. Debbie told me that several years ago, when she was at the mall, she happened to see Lesa. Lesa asked her if something was on her heart, and Debbie explained to her that she was struggling with the decision about leaving her nursing career and staying at home full-time with the children. Lesa said, "Let me send you something in the mail." As the story unfolds, when Lesa was praying about leaving her teaching job, she sat down and wrote the following. It helped her to process her decision, and as Debbie explained, it helped her to make a decision also. Enjoy!

**Lesa Gibson: Catching Acorns**

Two years ago I turned in *Julius Caesar* and my classroom and traded them for Dr. Suess and my laundry room. My second child was due in July, and after much prayer and contemplation, my husband and I agreed that my staying at home with our children would be in the best interest of everyone in the family.

This decision did not come easily. I had gone back to teaching when our first child was five months old. I loved teaching, but I knew the stresses of being a working mom–and that was with only one child at home. The thought of caring for an infant and a two-year-old *and* trying to fulfill my teaching responsibilities was a little overwhelming. Yet being a teacher was part of who I was. After all, God had undoubtedly called me to teach, hadn't he? Being a teacher had been my heart's desire since I was in the second grade! Now, was he calling me to come home?

The school board granted me a year's leave of absence, so we had those twelve months to ponder and pray whether that leave should be extended indefinitely. At first we wondered if we even had a choice. Our initial thoughts centered on money: Will we have enough? Are we being realistic to think we could really afford for me to stay at home? These and many other questions and anxieties would crowd my mind as I considered this life-changing move. But, as you will see, with each concern I silently voiced to our gracious heavenly Father, he responded clearly through his Word.

*1. Could we make ends meet financially?* After four years of marriage, my husband and I had established a two-income lifestyle. We had a house note, car note, utilities, insurance, groceries, diapers. Every time we attempted to balance his income with our outgo, we inevitably ended up with a negative number! It simply wouldn't work on paper. And God would respond: "I shall supply all your needs according to my riches in glory in Christ Jesus" (see Phil. 4:19).

And he has! We haven't missed a meal or a payment or a tithe in these two years, yet on paper it still doesn't work! Admittedly, our expenses are less–no child care, fewer fast-food meals, and I have a more "seasoned" wardrobe, but the basic truth is that God has provided. Indeed he is faithful even when our faith is dim.

*2. Would mothering full-time bring me the satisfaction and sense of accomplishment that teaching did?* I had taught high school English for ten years. My identity as "Mrs. Gibson" was much more comfortable and secure than my identity as "mom." I *knew* teaching and felt confident in my abilities. Although being a mother was definitely rewarding, I still second-guessed my methods and my competence. And God answered with his precious promises: "Like a shepherd He will tend His flock, In His arms He will gather the lambs, And carry *them* in His bosom; He will gently lead the nursing ewes" (Isa. 40:11 NASB). "Trust in the LORD with all your heart, And do not lean on your own understanding. In all your ways acknowledge him, and he will make your paths straight" (Prov. 3:5–6).

Wow, being "mom" has and continues to be more fulfilling and challenging than I ever imagined. The teachable moments that God provides while we're reading Bearenstain Bears books, playing Candyland, or just taking a stroll down the street are endless. I have come to realize that I am actually still teaching, only now my classroom is my home and my ultimate objective is clear—to recognize these children as precious gifts from God and to bring them up in the wisdom and admonition of the Lord. Certainly all days are not wonderful, but even on those days I hear his still small voice whispering, "This is where I need you right now."

*3. Would I be lonely?* Many of my closest friendships had developed within the circle of the school faculty. I had begun teaching there as a young single woman. These women had nurtured me, loved me, and coached me as I matured into marriage and motherhood. They were my cheerleaders, my encouragers, my supports. Indeed they were "family." Would I miss sharing daily conversation and coffee with them? And God whispered: "But seek first my kingdom and my righteousness; and all these things shall be added unto you" (Matt. 6:33 NASB).

And friends appeared, especially at church. I became involved in ministries and activities that I hadn't had time for when I was teaching—Baptist Young Women, Precepts Bible Studies, and teaching Mission Friends. All of these afforded me opportunities not only to grow in faith but also to make friends. These are heart friends who share the daily trials and triumphs of potty training, cutting teeth, and two-year-old tantrums. We encourage and listen and understand and pray as we travel through this same season of life together. God has drawn us to one another in the bonds of his love, and I have learned an even greater intimacy in my friendships with women. That is when we can come before God in prayer together.

*4. How would I feel about spending "Jim's" money?* We had always had one joint checking account; everything went into one pot dubbed "ours." Yet I began to wonder if I would ever feel comfortable buying something for myself without having contributed to "the pot." "And God is able to make all grace abound to you, so that in all things at all times, having all that you need, you will abound in every good work" (2 Cor. 9:8).

I truly believe that God has actually lessened my desire to have new "things" for myself. There is much more joy in spending *our* money on things for the whole family—bedding plants for the yard, Icees on hot summer days, and day trips to the beach. Having an understanding, loving husband has helped. He continues to reassure me that I am indeed contributing to the wealth of the family—perhaps not in coins but in immeasurable ways.

*5. Would I fall behind in my profession?* Education is an ever-changing, ever-growing field that requires keeping up with current issues, trends, and technology. I could continue reading my journals, but without practical application, could I stay abreast? "Be anxious for nothing, but in everything by prayer and supplication with thanksgiving let your requests be made known to God" (Phil. 4:6 NASB).

As he promised, I have been given opportunities to stay in touch with teaching through leading occasional staff development sessions, attending various workshops, and even now teaching a freshman English course at a local college. It has been in a spirit of thanksgiving that I have asked for these opportunities, grateful that God has gifted me with the desire and ability to teach. His faithfulness is boundless.

Ultimately our decision would be a harvest of our faith. God promised; we believed. His Word also says, "Without faith it is impossible to please Him, for he who comes to God must believe that He is and that He is a rewarder of those who seek Him" (Heb. 11:6 NASB). And my reward has been magnificent! My days have been filled with hugs and kisses and backyard baseball games and field trips around the neighborhood "catching" acorns beneath the giant oaks. Oh, there have been some refereeing, some "time-outs," and some tears, but I will forever be thankful that God has provided me with this opportunity that comes only once in a lifetime. As we are commanded to love the Lord our God with all our hearts and with all our souls and with all our mights, we are also called to teach these words diligently to our sons and talk of them when we sit in our house, and when we walk by the way and when we lie down and when we rise up (Deut. 6:7).

Indeed God's grace is infinite as he has enlightened the eyes of my heart, allowing himself to work in me and through me to accomplish his perfect will. Clearly I have come to realize that none of us are indispensable in the classroom, yet to our families we can be indispensable in our homes–beyond the laundry room. For you see, someone could use my old blackboard and my graffiti-carved podium and teach children about Atticus Finch and narrative essays. But who else could walk down the street holding the hands of my two little boys talking about God's love and catching acorns?

I wrote these words a little over seven years ago, and I am even more profoundly convinced of how right our decision was for me to stay at home. God has blessed us exceedingly abundantly, beyond all that we ever thought or imagined. He gave us a third son who will celebrate his fifth birthday this month, and I have continued to be able to stay at home. With this youngest child entering kindergarten in just a few months, I have done a lot of reflecting lately on my time at home with our boys. It has been absolutely incredible–exciting, exhausting, exhilarating, exasperating–and I wouldn't trade a day of it. To think I might have missed this–not just the joy of being with the children but the joy of seeing God's hand in so much of our lives, especially financially. At times his hands have been those of a church friend bringing a bag of hand-me-downs over just at the point when we realized someone's pants were getting a little snug. Other times his hands have been the mailman's when he brings an unexpected check for a utility or escrow refund just when we were wondering how we were going to make it that month. His hands have been evident in the handshake of Jim's boss, congratulating him on a job well done as he offered him a raise. Countless times through the years God has reminded us that he *will* provide for us if we will only trust him and allow him to.

God sent his Son so that we might experience a more abundant life. I have learned that his abundance is greater than anything I might have ever dreamed. Surely my cup runs over.

❧ Thank you, Lesa. I am confident that your story will help thousands of moms to process this important decision.

## Common Themes for Moms

After listening to these moms, let me summarize some of the common themes I heard:

1. Once you move from the workplace to the home place, be sure you plug into a network of other stay-at-home moms.
2. Keep a long-term, eternal perspective in life. This is a marathon not a sprint.
3. Use your time to plan and provide godly training for your children.
4. Remember, your attitude will end up affecting the entire family.
5. Be prepared to operate on a budget and be willing to sacrifice financially.

**Scripture to Ponder**

> Unless the LORD builds the house,
>  its builders labor in vain.
> Unless the LORD watches over the city,
>  the watchmen stand guard in vain.
> In vain you rise early
>  and stay up late,
> toiling for food to eat—
>  for he grants sleep to those he loves.
> Sons are a heritage from the Lord,
>  children a reward from him.

Like arrows in the hands of a warrior
   are sons born in one's youth.
Blessed is the man
   whose quiver is full of them.
They will not be put to shame
   when they contend with their enemies in the gate.

(Ps. 127:1–5)

**Action Step**

Pray and ask God to use the words of these moms to motivate and inspire you to accomplish your goal to stay at home.

CHAPTER 11

# Be Prepared

ETHAN

By failing to prepare, you are preparing to fail.
—Benjamin Franklin

To prepare for anything is simply to get ready. Before a runner begins the race, he trains for hours. Before an army goes to war, they develop their strategies and back-up contingencies. Before a football team takes the field, they carefully analyze their opponents and prepare their game plan. Before an airplane pilot flies a plane, he goes through a series of checklists to be sure the plane is ready for takeoff. And finally, before a mom quits her job, she had better prepare for this major transition in her family.

In chapters 6, 7, and 8, I gave you "Your Road Map to Success," a five-step plan to get you home. These five action steps are the keys to your preparation and transition. I want to emphasize again that using a Money Allocation Plan is the key to your long-term success. Yes, the ability for you to get home and remain at home will be based on how you manage your money on a daily basis.

If you are following the recommended plan, you have spent (or you are in the process of spending) thirty days meditating on Scripture and preparing spiritually. You have confirmed the priorities in your life, spent hours and hours carefully analyzing your income and expenses (line by line), and trimmed your expenses so they would not exceed your income. And you are beginning to use a Money Allocation Plan (MAP) each month.

This is the process you must go through to accomplish your goal! There are no shortcuts to this process.

On the pages that follow in this chapter, I hope to provide you with numerous straightforward summary ideas already presented in previous chapters on how to prepare for your transition home. Many of these ideas come from over fifteen years of financial advising and the numerous stay-at-home moms that I have talked with over the years.

Listed below are twenty-five summary key concepts to help you move from the marketplace to the home place.

1. Be prepared spiritually. Spend time in God's Word daily and be faithful to pray for yourself and your family.
2. List your written goals and priorities on paper.
3. Carefully develop your new MAP (budget) for one income.
4. Update and monitor your budget every week to be sure you are living within your means.
5. Ask a friend to keep you accountable to live on your new budget (MAP).
6. Don't make costly mistakes that could end up jeopardizing your plan and forcing you to go back to work.
7. Look for creative ways to cut every expense possible.
8. Live on one income for six months before you quit your job.
9. During this six-month period, save your income (mom) and establish a crisis fund/emergency fund for your family that will be available to meet unexpected expenses after you are home and living on one income.
10. Develop a plan to pay off all consumer debt as fast as possible. It will be easier to live on one income if you do not have any consumer debt obligations. Let me recommend a nonprofit counseling service that can help you get organized and pay off all your consumer debts: Consumer Credit Counseling Services (CCCS). Check your local phone book for an office in your city.
11. Do not use credit cards during your transition period. Pay for everything with cash.

12. Always pay your credit card bills in full every month. This will keep you out of a financial crisis due to credit card debt.
13. Keep supporting God's kingdom. Don't become a token giver and rob God.
14. During your time of transition, do not make any major purchases like a new home or new car.
15. Be sure the husband has no plans of changing jobs during this transition time in your family.
16. Don't worry about what everybody else is buying or doing. Remember the priorities for your family.
17. Learn to be content. A lot of people will have more material possessions than you do, so don't let greed or envy affect your attitude.
18. As one mom told me, "Stay out of the car. Because every time you get in the car, you usually spend money."
19. Work hard at carefully managing your money!
20. Be prepared emotionally as you enter into a new routine and lifestyle.
21. Maximize your time and schedule now that you are home.
22. Develop a network with other moms at home for encouragement during this time of transition.
23. Consider a home-based business if additional income is necessary.
24. Maintain your eternal perspective every day! Remember, being a stay-at-home mom is a marathon, not a sprint.
25. Have a thankful heart.

I am confident that if anyone will work on doing the things listed above, they will find success. Don't let this list overwhelm you, but simply view it as a reminder of how you can accomplish and maintain your goal of staying at home.

**Scripture to Ponder**

"Not that I speak from want; for I have learned to be content in whatever circumstances I am. I know how to get along with humble means, and I also know how to live in prosperity; in any and every circumstance I have learned the secret of being filled and going hungry, both of having abundance and suffering need. I can do all things through Him who strengthens me" (Phil. 4:11–13 NASB).

**Action Step**

Review the summary key concepts in this chapter and see how you are doing. Are you on track to accomplish your goal, or do you need to make some changes based upon this summary list?

## CHAPTER 12

# Mary Talks to Moms

We've conquered outer space, but not inner space.
We've cleaned up the soil but polluted the soul. . . .
We have fancier houses, but more broken homes.

I love Paul's words in Philippians 3:13b-14: "Forgetting what is behind and straining toward what is ahead, I press on toward the goal to win the prize for which God has called me heavenward in Christ Jesus."

Paul did not say, "Remembering the past and wondering how life would have been if only . . ."

As I have grown older and better understand the sovereignty of God, I can truly rest in Jesus Christ knowing that he has allowed whatever has happened in my life. Yes, the good, the bad, and even the *if onlys*. I find so much comfort and strength in the words of Romans 8:28, "And we know that in all things God works for the good of those who love him, who have been called according to his purpose."

Mom, that verse tells you and me that God is in the business of turning "spilled paint" into his perfect rainbows. Isn't that exciting!

As much as I hate to admit it, before long I will pass the half-century mark. I imagine that I am older than you are, and I want to write this chapter from my heart to your heart.

Would I do things differently if I could somehow be a twenty-three-year old bride once again? Knowing what I know now–yes, I would have done many things differently! But I did not know then what I know now. I really have no business wishing for what was not.

I think you will find the following statistics from *Leadership* magazine interesting:

Percentage of age group of people who, if they could start over in life, would do things "much differently":[1]

| | ages | | |
|---|---|---|---|
| | 16–31 | 59% |
| | 32–50 | 71% |
| | 51+ | 59% |

As a Christian, it is so comforting to know that God indeed does work every single thing for good when I love him and want to accomplish his perfect will in my life. But I need to press forward to whatever God has for me today.

One of the many things I did not really grasp when I was young is that little decisions make a big difference! I can still recall a discussion that Jim and I had when Chris was an infant. I had initially quit work to be a stay-at-home mom. At the same time Jim quit his salaried job to become self-employed in the insurance business. Jim and I were optimistic people, and life had always somehow seemed to work out for us, so we just assumed this would also work out. (And, of course, we did not have a budget or a crisis fund.)

Chris was born two months prematurely, cash flow was short, and our second car up and died on us. It was my idea (Yes, my idea–I am indeed a descendent of Adam and Eve!) to go back to work part-time so we could purchase a second (used) car. I have thought many times about that decision. Today Jim and I agree that we would have chosen sharing one car if we could somehow relive that early decision.

Also, we did not comprehend the real cost of compounding interest. It was stated in *USA Today*: "Suppose you have a $3,000 balance on a credit card that charges you 19.8% interest, and you pay only the required minimum balance of $15 a month. It would take 39 years to pay off that $3,000, and you would pay more than $10,000 in interest."[2] Wow!

Well, compare the decision for me to go back to work part-time to pay for a car with what I was claiming was my desire. I wanted to be a stay-at-home mom. But what did my actions say was more important? Staying home or having a second car? As much as I hate to admit it, you and I both know the vote I took the day I went back to work: it was for the car.

But I rationalized, I was not going to work for long! Soon I'd be back home!

But . . . but . . .

Do you know how expensive medical bills can be? And then our second child came . . . and kindergarten–a private, Christian school at that. And, of course, the house was too small, and we had to move into a larger home.

Just a little decision to go back to work for just a little while–part-time.

I truly believe that God is taking some of Jim and my mistakes and using them as examples for you. He is working our past mistakes for good. God is so faithful! He uses our regrets for his good and multiplies our faithfulness–even in the little things.

I recently read in the *Arkansas Democrat-Gazette*:

> Many Americans think they stand a better chance of getting rich from lotteries or sweepstakes than from saving and investing, a poll found.
>
> Stephen Brobeck, executive director of the Consumer Federation of America, said the findings suggest that people don't know that small amounts of money can grow if saved or invested. That may be preventing some people from trying to improve their lot, Brobeck said.
>
> Meanwhile, a telephone poll of 1,010 Americans 18 and older conducted July 22 to July 25 found that most Americans undervalue savings. People were asked, for example, how much $25 invested weekly for 40 years at 7 percent annual yield would amount to.
>
> Less than a third guessed more than $150,000. The correct answer is $286,640.[3]

Mom, if you really want to be home with your kids, I suggest that you follow Ethan's advice in this book. Proverbs 15:22 reminds us, "Plans fail for lack of counsel, but with many advisers they succeed."

You are taking the right step to seek sound, biblically based financial advice in your quest to return home.

Also, ask God to show you how you can be the best mom possible in your particular situation and how you can understand the unique bent of each of your children. FamilyLife, a division of Campus Crusade for Christ, not only has an outstanding marriage conference but also an excellent parenting conference. The following information (adapted from the appendix of the *FamilyLife Parenting Conference Manual*[4]) will help you realize the challenging job you have as a mom. Your relationship with your children is key as they learn to trust, develop self-confidence, understand rules and roles, and more!

## CHILD'S AGE AND CHARACTERISTICS

**0–18 months:** This is the "being and doing" stage, in which the child decides to BE (live and thrive), decides to TRUST, and chooses to creatively EXPLORE his world.

**18 months–3 years:** This also is an important stage for developing self-confidence and for learning boundaries to his growing independence. He'll begin to develop his sense of self, learning from every experience.

**3–6 years:** The preschool years are "magical" for children. Their abilities to create and imagine begin to blossom and are delightful to observe. Also emerging is the child's identity–sexual and social–that is formed through experimentation with rules and roles for behavior.

Barbara Curtis certainly understands the importance of motherhood! She shares a wonderful chart in her book *Small Beginnings: First Steps to Prepare Your Child for Lifelong Learning.*[5] Her chart will help you recognize some specific ways that you can help your children learn and grow (see page 132).

Mom, you are so important!

## Five Potentials for Joyful Lifelong Learning*

| Toddler Potential | Ready Signals | Reinforcement | Short-Term Benefit | Long-Term Benefit |
|---|---|---|---|---|
| INDEPENDENCE "I can do it!" | Seeking self-reliance; Frustration | Make doing possible; Extra time; Extra care; Different approach | Satisfaction | Confidence |
| ORDER "Where does it (where do I) belong?" | Stacking objects; Closing doors and drawers | Child-friendly environment; A place for everything; Sequencing | Security | Efficiency |
| SELF CONTROL "What are by limits?" | Imitating adults, e.g., at prayer; Ability to hold still for short periods | Gross motor challenges: Walking on line; Walking with bell; Tuning into silence; Small Beginnings exercise | Peace | Well-being |
| CONCENTRATION "Quiet! Mind at work!" | Examining small objects; Absorption in any specific activity | Observe what clicks; Invite repetition | Ability to learn | Productivity |
| SERVICE "Let me help!" | Desire to participate in household chores | Share housework; Accept results; Encourage and praise | Self-worth | Meaningful life |

*Barbara Curtis, *Small Beginnings* (Nashville: Broadman & Holman Publishers, 1997), p. 37.

*USA Today* reported:

> The more hours a young child spends in child care, the less apt mom and child are to be attuned to each other, new government research says.
>
> The study finds a "small but significant" link between child care up to age 3 and somewhat poorer mother-child interaction. Both the mother's "sensitivity" toward her child–how "in tune" she is with the child–and her child's engagement with her are affected, according to findings reported in *Developmental Psychology*, published by the American Psychological Association.[6]

I don't share these to put you (or me) on a guilt trip. Remember, God is sovereign. We will press forward, right? I share this information because our kids need us, and all moms are really important–not only to their own children but actually to the world!

OK, since we are having a heart-to-heart talk, I have one last thing to share with you: Don't nag your husband about wanting to stay at home. (I have personal experience in this.)

First, give your desires to the Lord. Second, prayerfully discuss the situation with your husband and seek godly advice. Third, wait on the Lord and trust him to lead your husband and you . . . in his time . . . in his way.

I confess, I used to complain to Jim frequently that I wanted to stay at home. I recently asked him how it made him feel:

"Well," he said, "it made me angry because I was working as hard as I could possibly work, and I was not in a salaried position. . . . While it was a noble desire for you to stay home, I had little control over how realistic it was financially. I also recognized that I had made some mistakes and was paying for those mistakes economically. Until we could overcome those obstacles, staying home was not realistic. And it was very frustrating to be in my position."

I asked Jim what advice he has for you: "I would sit down with someone who could be objective. Too often it is easy to attach emotional value to some things that we might just as well to do without.

"Also, the best way to insure that the wife can stay at home is to make a plan for that day. Don't wait until the kids are in private schools, you have a larger mortgage, and need to replace the car. And prepare your kids to think about finances."

Share Jim's advice with your spouse. Personally, I think it is very good.

Yes, Jim and I have made some poor financial decisions. But I think we have done a good job preparing our children about finances. We have shared our regrets with them as well as what God's Word says about debt.

Our oldest son, Chris, really wanted to go to a certain private, Christian college. We prayed and asked the Lord to provide a good scholarship if this was his will, and the scholarship just did not materialize. We did not want to take a loan to pay for Chris's college education, nor did we think that it would be a good idea for Chris to do this. He reluctantly obeyed us and attended a public university.

Chris is now a senior at Arkansas State University, and it is easy to clearly see that ASU was God's perfect choice for Chris. He has had many, many opportunities at ASU to grow spiritually and mentally. He met his bride-to-be and has been mentored by some godly men. Chris and his fiancée are now talking about going to either the mission field or to seminary. I am so very glad that he is not graduating with a $40,000 student loan! And God used his "no" to lead Chris to what I believe was his perfect "yes"!

Let me close with portions of what is called "A Modern Paradox." I read it in an editorial by John R. Starr. He explained that he retrieved it from the Internet and did not know the author.

The paradox of our time in history is that we have taller buildings but shorter tempers. We buy more but enjoy it less.

We have bigger houses and smaller families; more conveniences but less time; more degrees but less sense; more experts, but also more problems.

We have multiplied our possession but reduced our values. We talk too much, love too seldom, and hate too often. We have learned how to make a living, but not a life.

We've been to the moon and back but have trouble crossing the street to meet a new neighbor. We've conquered outer space, but not inner space.

We've cleaned up the soil but polluted the soul. . . . We have fancier houses, but more broken homes.[7]

Mom, Jesus promises tells us in Hebrews 13:8 that "Jesus Christ is the same yesterday and today and forever." Although our times have changed, our Savior has not. He can help us restore our values and reclaim our homes. His Word never changes, and his way is right and good!

## Scriptures to Ponder

"Forgetting what is behind and straining toward what is ahead, I press on toward the goal to win the prize for which God has called me heavenward in Christ Jesus" (Phil. 3:13b–14).

"Forget the former things; do not dwell on the past. See, I am doing a new thing! Now it springs up; do you not perceive it! I am making a way in the desert and streams in the wasteland" (Isa. 43:18–19).

"If any of you lacks wisdom, he should ask God, who gives generously to all without finding fault, and it will be given to him" (James 1:5).

## Action Steps

1. With your spouse (if single, do this with a close female friend), jot on a sheet of paper some of your past mistakes. Pray together that the Lord will use each of these mistakes for good, and then tear up the sheet of paper and throw it away.

2. Pray with your spouse or friend for God's perfect wisdom concerning your situation. Jot down any thoughts the Lord brings to your mind about it.

# CHAPTER 13
## Ethan Talks to Dads

*Fear knocked at the door, faith answered, and no one was there.*

Dad, I have been pondering for several weeks what God would have me write to you. This is a special chapter to me because most moms reading this book have already settled the issue about staying at home or leaving the workplace and coming home. I have to assume that you agree with your wife.

Since this book was not written to "convince" anyone to have mom stay at home, I am not going to address you in a "convincing" style but with an attitude of encouragement and compassion. I know the feelings you and your wife are having right now. You are struggling with the questions: How are we going to make it financially? Will we have to move to a smaller house? What about our cars? How will our children respond when our family has less money to spend? Are we really doing the right thing? What are our friends going to think if we have to lower our lifestyle? Can I handle the pressure? I would be concerned if you were not asking these questions because this would show a lack of leadership and maturity in your life.

As a husband and as a dad, I would like to address four issues with you in this chapter. They involve faith, leadership, priorities, and perseverance. Yes, as Christians we live a life of faith. One of my favorite sayings from Dave Johnson's *Success Principle* has been, "Fear knocked at the door, faith answered, but no one was there!" Be sure that you are responding to any fear in your life with biblical faith.

## FAITH

Even when we are living a life of faith, God's Word exhorts us to be wise and plan ahead. "For which one of you, when he wants to build a tower, does not first sit down and calculate the cost, to see if he has enough to complete it? Otherwise, when he has laid a foundation, and is not able to finish, all who observe it begin to ridicule him, saying, 'This man began to build and was not able to finish.'" (Luke 14:28–30 NASB). Do not be deceived; just because you are planning and counting the cost does not mean that you are not living a life of biblical faith!

"What is faith? It is the confident assurance that what we hope for is going to happen. It is the evidence of things we cannot yet see" (Heb. 11:1 NLT). The Christian life is a life of faith. Do you believe there is a God who created the universe? If you do, can you trust him to provide for the spiritual, financial, and emotional needs of your family? Absolutely yes! Ask God to put within your heart the faith to believe that everything you are attempting to accomplish will bring glory to him. Let me encourage you to take one step of faith at a time.

## LEADERSHIP

At critical decision-making times like this your family needs a captain—one who will take charge, stand tall, and be the leader God has called you to be! It's easy to be the captain of the ship when the water is calm, but what kind of captain are you when the waters are rough? To be honest, there are usually some significant trials during any transition. This is when God expects you to be strong and lead your family through the storm.

In my time with the Lord this morning, I was reading in 1 Corinthians 16:13–14. I have read this passage numerous times, but I believe I read it with a different perspective today—mainly because this was the day I had planned to work on my chapter to dads. This is what it says: "Be on the alert, stand firm in the faith, act like men, be strong. Let all that you do be done in love" (NASB). What tremendous words of wisdom for us as dads!

The NIV puts verse 13 this way: "Be on your guard; . . . be men of courage." The NKJV used the words, "be brave, be strong." The NLT says, "Be on guard. Stand true to what you believe. Be courageous. Be strong." Wow! I love this exhortation from the Word of God! This is exactly what we need to be doing as men and leaders of our family. I know from personal experience as a man that it is not always easy to stand tall and have courage. Sometimes it is tough to make the hard decisions, but God will give us the strength we need!

I remember I was faced with making a major decision several years ago. It would affect my family, our finances, and our future. While driving my car one day, the Lord impressed this thought in my heart: "Ethan, life is too short, and eternity is too long, not to be making the right decisions today." That was all the Lord needed to tell me in order for me to make the right decision.

My encouragement to you is to fulfill the God-given role in your family. Don't tell your wife to figure out if your family can live on one income, but you take the leadership and work with your wife on your new Money Allocation Plan (budget). You be the one who brings a sense of confidence to the family as you move into uncharted waters. You be the one to take your wife by the hand and pray together about this decision and ask God for wisdom. You be the one to get on your knees and ask God to provide for your family. You be the one to explain the coming changes in the family to your children.

Let me also encourage you to form an accountability group with other dads who are praying about getting mom home. Pray and be an encouragement to each other on a regular basis.

## PRIORITIES

In addition to exhorting you to have faith and be the leader of your family, I feel like I need to address another issue in this chapter. This book talks a lot about moms being at home and raising the children. I can assure you that no one is better equipped to nurture and care for the children than a mom. However, helping to raise the children is also your responsibility as a dad! Just because you are the financial provider for the family and work outside the home does not exempt you from your role of being a dad.

Unfortunately, some dads delegate 100 percent of the child raising to the mom and feel absolutely no responsibility to help out. Your children need time with you. Your children need to have you around the house when you are not working. Your wife needs your help (and a break from watching the children twenty-four hours every day). If you are not spending time with your children on a regular basis, let me exhort you to examine your priorities and begin to make some changes today.

## PERSEVERANCE

Finally, as one dad to another, I would like to encourage you to persevere! I realize it's tough to hang in there over the long haul. It's tough when you have to take one car to the repair shop and drop off the other car for repairs as you are picking the first one up. (This has happened to me more times than I would like to remember.) Have you ever heard the joke, You know it's going to be a tough day when . . . you walk into your office and see Mike Wallace with *60 Minutes* sitting in your waiting room. Well, you know things have been going badly when you don't need a phone book to look up your plumber's phone number. It's tough when you work all week and have to come home and cut the grass, repair the roof, and find a stack of bills that need to be paid. One of our goals as a dad should be to model perseverance.

As an alumni of Dallas Theological Seminary, I receive the DTS *Dallas Connection* alumni newsletter. In the 1998 winter issue, Doug Cecil, director of alumni relations, wrote this article. I trust it will be an encouragement in your life.

In 1972, I bought my Oldsmobile Cutlass brand new off a lot in Cincinnati, Ohio. At the time, I thought it was a rip-off to pay $3,600 for the vehicle. But I still drive the beast! It has a 350 V-8 engine that eats gas like crazy and a great rumble sound that might challenge Chuck's Harley. Over 200,000 miles later, the smell of exhaust still does wonders for my psyche! And, now that it has celebrated its 25th anniversary, maybe I have gotten my money's worth.

That car has been with me through thick and thin. It has lived in Ohio, Michigan, California, and Texas. It was around before my kids. Our family even grew so close to this crazy vehicle that we gave it the name "Chip." (Actually the original name was "Chocolate Chip" due to the color scheme of the car.) Now, I mention this because over the years, Chip has become a visible reminder of faithfulness to me. I know that not everyone has been as fortunate with cars, but this one has been reliable and faithful transportation. Chip has served us well. And you may laugh at me, but at least it is still running! William Carey, the great missionary to India, wrote, "If, after my removal, any one should think it worth his while to write my life, I will give you a criteria by which you may judge of its correctness. If he gave me credit for being a plodder, he will describe me justly. Anything beyond this will be too much. I can plod. I can persevere in any definite pursuit. To this I owe everything." I can do that! I can plod. I can hang in there. Like Chip, I might cough and wheeze a little, but I can keep on going. For me, desirable characteristics like faithfulness and consistency in ministry come to mind and encourage me to press on. Proverbs 3:3 says, "Let love and faithfulness never leave you; bind them around your neck, write them on the tablet of your heart." Oftentimes in ministry (life) there is a temptation to retreat rather than to persevere. The tendency is to give up when the going gets tough rather than work through the difficulties. For William Carey, I am sure the pressures of ministry in India were great, yet he kept plodding. For us, the pressures may come through a variety of forms, but the feelings are the same. Maybe you feel the temptation to quit. Be faithful! Keep plodding.[1]

For over three years now I have had this article propped up on the top of a bookcase in my office. I guess one of the reasons it means so much to me is that after my wife, Janet, read the article, she wrote the following words at the bottom of the article. "Ethan Pope, a more faithful man, I've never known. JP" Even though I have told her how much that meant to me, she will never know how God has used those nine words in my life. It's not just the words that are important to me. What makes them important in my life is the person who wrote them!

As one dad to another, let me encourage you to live a life of faith, be the leader of your family, establish the right priorities with your time, and keep on plodding! Therefore, when you stand before the Lord and give an accounting of your life, you will hear the words, "A job well done, thou good and faithful dad." Plod on my friend; never give up!

## Scripture to Ponder

"Be on the alert, stand firm in the faith, act like men, be strong. Let all that you do be done in love" (1 Cor. 16:13–14 NASB).

## Action Steps

1. Recruit some other dads to pray with you on a regular basis.

2. Take charge of this transition time in your family. Be the leader God has called you to be.

## CHAPTER 14

# Home-Based Career Options

## MARY

*Love is the master key to a happy home.*

*–Anonymous*

We live in an age when literally millions of people work from home. Actually, "about one-third of Americans work from a home office, and ongoing technological developments ensure the number will rise. . . .

"'For many, the decision to have a home office is a lifestyle consideration,' she [Kim Gordon, president of the National Marketing Federations, Inc.] says. 'You can be available to your family.'"[1]

I have friends who have worked from home typing medical records, teaching piano lessons, writing, taking care of others' children, making crafts, and doing graphic artwork. With the technological advances today, many companies are welcoming home employment.

As I was researching home careers for this chapter, I discovered a site by Hartman Research Group. It stated:

> As we move into the new millennium, more corporations are embracing the "work from home" ideal. They have come to realize that there are billions of dollars to be saved by keeping their employees at home. Not only is much saved in the office building itself (heat, electricity, etc.), but most find that their employees are more productive without the pressures of the office.

There is almost no aspect in the running of major corporations that cannot be done, at least partially, in a home office situation. Companies are shifting away from hiring hourly office help to do such things as word processing.

With today's technology, it can be done at home, then faxed or mailed to the office. Depending upon your post with the company, you may be required to physically check in a couple times a week, or you may not.

This particular site had a listing of home employment opportunities. I am sure that there are other such resources available that are free for the asking.

Think of your friends and associates. I imagine that you have some who are working out of their homes right now. Ask them how they began and what suggestions they would have for you.

I took a leave of absence to write my first book, *My Heart's at Home!* I loved being at home and the added flexibility it gave me for meeting the needs of my family. As our children were in school at that time, I wrote while they were away from home. Often I would rise early in the morning to write, when the house was quiet and I would not have any interruptions.

The key to your success in any home career is discipline. If you want to write, you have to write. If you want to teach children how to play the piano, you have to schedule the time to do this. Having a home business takes the entire family's cooperation. If you have small children, you may find that you can work only a few hours a day from home while the children are still asleep or taking naps.

Just remember that God calls you and me, as women, to love our husbands and nurture our families. And just because we are at home does not mean that we are fulfilling our roles. Even if we are full-time stay-at-home moms, you and I both know that we can be pulled by the tug of church, community activities, hobbies, and a myriad of other things. Since you want to work at home in order to focus on your family, be sure that you have a plan for doing just that! It is entirely possible to be disconnected from our families even though we are physically at home. If family is our priority, we have to be sure that we make it our priority.

*Small Time Operator* suggests that a service business is the easiest to set up. It states: "The owner of a service business is also more likely to be subject to state licenses and regulations.

"If you do something well—fixing things, painting or decorating, writing or editing, cutting hair, operating a computer—these are but a few possibilities for your own service business. And if you are good at something, you might consider teaching those skills to others. Be imaginative. Don't ignore your own resources."[2]

Mom, I think the reminder that we should not ignore our own resources is good advice. Psalm 139:14 tells us that we are "fearfully and wonderfully made." The Lord gave you and me special talents and gifts that he wants us to use to bring glory to God.

You must ask yourself several questions if you choose to work at home: What practical steps can I take to be sure that working at home allows me to focus on my family rather than distract me from my responsibilities? How many hours a day will I commit to working? Prayerfully discuss these matters with your spouse.

My favorite time to work at home is when everyone is still asleep. I enjoy rising early and having a quiet house to myself, and this does not distract from family responsibilities. If you have school-age children, you may want to consider using the time when they are away from school as your time to work. This may or may not be a practical solution for you, depending on the type of work you choose to do.

One of my friends teaches piano. As most of her students are children, she teaches them after her own children have arrived home from school. She has found it best to teach her pupils on two specific afternoons a week to free her up for the remainder of the week. She takes the same holidays as her children—summers, Thanksgiving week, and two weeks at Christmas. Parents registering their children for piano lessons know this up front. She also asks them to commit to take lessons for an entire school year.

It is obvious that my friend and her husband thought through the ramifications of a home-based business and how it would affect their family. Planning ahead has allowed her the flexibility she needs to focus on those she loves while using the talents God has given her.

You need to ask yourself why you are working in the first place and how many hours you feel God would desire you to work. Everyone's situation is so different!

For example, you and your spouse may believe that God wants you to send your children to a Christian school and that he would be pleased for you to use some of your skills to help with the financial aspects of this. You and your spouse may decide that being a home-school teacher is the work that God has called you to do instead of Christian education. You might not receive an actual paycheck, but it's definitely working at home. I believe that each family should bring their unique situation before the Lord and that as Christians, we do not need to judge one another.

After all, God calls you and me first to love him so that his love may overflow into our love for our families. That's exactly what the woman in Proverbs 31 did.

> She selects wool and flax and works with eager hands.
> She is like the merchant ships bringing her food from afar.
> She gets up while it is still dark; she provides food for her
> family and portions for her servant girls. She considers a field
> and buys it; out of her earning she plants a vineyard. She sets
> about her work vigorously; her arms are strong for her tasks.
> She sees that her trading is profitable, and her lamp does not
> go out at night. In her hand she holds the distaff and grasps
> the spindle with her fingers. . . . She makes linen garments
> and sells them, and supplies the merchants with sashes
> (Prov. 31:13–19, 24).

My, this woman was not bored!

And, in verses 27–28, we are reminded: "She watches over the affairs of her household. . . . Her children arise and call her blessed; her husband also, and he praises her."

The Proverbs 31 woman was not working just to be working. She was looking after the affairs of her household–with her husband's blessing. It is evident that her heart was right as she worked because her husband and children called her blessed. May you and I follow her example of fearing God and being committed to our loved ones.

The New Testament (Acts 16:14) tells us that Lydia was "a dealer in purple cloth from the city of Thyatira, who was a worshiper of God." I find it interesting that "Thyatira was famous for its cloth dyers, so we assume that Lydia dealt in cloth of purple and possibly in the dye itself."[3]

You are probably familiar with the biblical account of Nehemiah and how he was used by God to rebuild the ruined wall that surrounded Jerusalem. We are told in Nehemiah 3:12, "Shallum son of Hallohesh, ruler of a half-district of Jerusalem, repaired the next section with the help of his daughters." These young women undoubtedly worked hard to help their dad and to bring glory to God.

You may have doubts about whether you could work from home. Maybe you have been told that you just don't have what it takes. Let me encourage you with some true stories about some people who were told that they would not make it:

After Fred Astaire's first screen test, a 1933 memo from the MGM testing director said: "Can't act. Slightly bald. Can dance a little." Astaire kept that memo over the fireplace in his Beverly Hills home.

An expert said of famous football coach Vince Lombardi: "He possesses minimal football knowledge. Lacks motivation."

Louisa May Alcott, the author of *Little Women*, was advised by her family to find work as a servant or seamstress.

Beethoven handled the violin awkwardly and preferred playing his own compositions instead of improving his technique. His teacher called him hopeless as a composer.

The teacher of famous opera singer Enrico Caruso said Caruso had no voice at all and could not sing.

Walt Disney was fired by a newspaper for lacking ideas. He also went bankrupt several times before he built Disneyland.[4]

Now, let's see what God tells you in Proverbs 2:6–8: "For the LORD gives wisdom, and from his mouth come knowledge and understanding. He holds victory in store for the upright, he is a shield to those whose walk is blameless, for he guards the course of the just and protects the way of his faithful ones."

May God give you discernment and his perfect wisdom in deciding if a home-based occupation is right for you and your family. And no matter how he leads you, may your heart be at home with those you love!

### Scriptures to Ponder

"If God is for us, who is against us?" (Rom. 8:31 NASB).

"Teach me good discernment and knowledge, For I believe in Thy commandments" (Ps. 119:66 NASB).

### Action Steps

1. (Discuss with your spouse, if you are married.) Why or why not do you feel that a home-based occupation would be right (not right) for you? Write down your thoughts on a separate piece of paper.

2. Also, list some of the unique talents God has given you. Brainstorm with your spouse (or a friend of the same sex if not married) and determine if any of these talents could be used in a home-based career.

3. Jot down several action points. For example, if you believe that God is using you to teach piano lessons in your home, talk with someone who does this. Also, if you will need to scale back living expenses to exchange your office occupation for a home-based occupation, list specific areas where you could cut back.

## CHAPTER 15

# Testimonies of God's Provision

## ETHAN

Trust in the Lord with all your heart,
And do not lean on your own understanding.
In all your ways acknowledge Him,
And He will make your paths straight.

                            –Proverbs 3:5–6 NASB

## GOD IS FAITHFUL!

On the pages that follow you will be reading real testimonies written by real people about how God has provided for their family. For every testimony you read in this chapter, there are thousands of others who also have a story to tell about God's provision. During the last few months I received numerous written testimonies from across the nation. It is unfortunate that I could not reprint all of them because each one demonstrated the faithfulness of God. In fact, some of the ones printed below had to be condensed and edited for this chapter. Go ahead and make a fresh cup of coffee, sit back in your favorite chair, and be prepared for God to bless your life!

## CAROLE TILLMAN

My husband and I made choices many years ago that put us in the unique position of seeing God provide miraculously. I have been home since our seven children began arriving fifteen years ago. We are also committed not to have any debt outside of our mortgage. We have been given two vehicles to accommodate our growing family, a week's vacation in a time-share condo in Florida, and been the grateful recipients of many free or discounted goods and services from business and professional people who just wanted to bless us. But two years ago my husband lost his full-time ministry position and had to begin supplementing our income with a second job. Like no other time in our lives, we have seen God faithfully provide for our needs.

As people began to hear of our situation, unsolicited cash gifts began to arrive at our doorstep. One time a man we hardly know came to our door and gave us five one-hundred-dollar bills in a Christmas card. A group of men that knew my husband through the YMCA's Indian Princess Program gave us $600 to help meet a mortgage payment. A fellow believer called one night to say he and his wife wanted to make a couple of our mortgage payments for us so we would not feel pressured to take the first job that became available. He said he wanted us to be able to wait for God's best and take some of the financial pressure off of us. Three $1,000 gifts were given anonymously through our church's benevolence program. One couple bought groceries and gave us $100 in gift certificates for a grocery store. Christmas gifts were left anonymously wrapped on our doorstep.

For the first three months after our layoff, our income was actually higher than if Walter had still been working full-time at his old job. We began to make mortgage payments ahead of schedule and were three months ahead of schedule at one point.

May 1999 brought us another opportunity to see God come through as Jehovah-Jirah. We were still limping along financially from the layoff eighteen months before when we received a much shorter than expected paycheck from the faith-based ministry where we had begun to work. We only had $109 with which to make all of our monthly obligations. That was not even enough to feed our family of nine until the next paycheck arrived. My usually stalwart faith was crumbling. I needed a renewed word from him that we were still on track.

One morning I cried out to God and asked him please to encourage me that day. Later that morning a friend took me to a state homeschooling convention. She gave me $50 and said for me to spend it however I wished. While there I talked with a homeschooling vendor who lived absolutely by faith. Their only income was from their sales and whatever God prompted others to give them. Their family of five lived in a motor home and traveled all over the country. I shared my story with him, and he encouraged me from Daniel 3, saying to trust God even if he didn't deliver me. "God will send ravens from heaven to feed you if he has to; trust him." I told him he had given me what I came for and gave him my $50 as a demonstration of my appreciation and trust for God.

The next week, at 4:45 A.M. on May 26, I was returning to bed after taking care of our baby. I felt prompted to turn on my bedside light. When I did, I found my Bible lying open to Proverbs 27:27, where I had previously marked this verse with "God will provide" in the margin. I reread this promise: "And there will be goats' milk enough for your food, for the food of your household, and sustenance for your maidens." My anxiety vanished, and I fell peacefully back to sleep.

On May 27, a friend came by with a check for $250 and said she and her husband had just felt prompted to do this for us. Two other friends gave us $100 each. The next day a fourth friend dropped by with $200, lasagna for supper, and clothes exactly my size, style, and color! There were so many clothes, I emptied my closet, replacing many of my older clothes with her things and still had a huge box that I was able to mail to another friend who also needed clothes. God not only provided for me but allowed me the privilege of giving to someone else's need.

This past Christmas we saw another outpouring of God's provision. A relative gave our family a new computer, printer, and Internet service for a year. We were able to buy a rolltop desk for the computer with other Christmas cash gifts we received. A family in our church anonymously sent us each individual Christmas presents. My neighbor, who usually buys each of my children a gift, instead gave me $150 for me to buy them for her. I was able to get gifts I couldn't afford to get myself in her name!

The gift I have appreciated the most, though, is the gift of his presence. Without fail he sends me encouragement through his Word or the word of a friend. I know my phone will ring with an encouraging word from a friend when I get discouraged. It's happened too consistently just to be coincidence.

## ANGELA ANDERSON

I loved my job. I was good at it, and I was successful. I was in the right place at the right time, worked hard, and did well. Now I am not talking about one of these dot-com companies where I became a millionaire in two years. This was an old-fashion Fortune 500 company. Good benefits and pension. A place where you could stay for your career.

But my husband and I decided long before we got married that I would stay at home if we had children. Our first child arrived two weeks before his graduation from graduate school. Instead of following our long-term plan, my husband and I agreed that he should pursue his dream and passion of writing. He would stay at home with our newborn and pursue a freelance writing career while I continued paying the bills at my job.

Eighteen months later I was pregnant with our second child, and the writing assignments were not rolling in as we had dreamed. My desire to be at home with our son was increasing. In a week of defining moments, the ultimate role reversal took place in our home. I entertained clients in a skybox at Texas Stadium for a Monday night football game, had a huge steak dinner, and played (yes, pregnant) in a golf tournament.

The next day my husband started working on his resume. It was a huge struggle. He did not pursue using the graduate degree he just completed. He had been freelancing for one and one-half years, which translates as unemployed to a lot of folks. And we prayed. He pursued every lead he could. God had miraculously provided me with this blossoming career from the want ads of the *Dallas Morning*

*News.* God had also given me wisdom in declining a position more up my alley where layoffs had taken place a year or so later.

We trusted God. We believed in him to be our Jehovah Jirah, our Provider. The reality of our modest mortgage payment and growing family looked impossible to me. At Christmastime my husband asked my father for a position in his North Carolina company. To my shock and dismay, my father said no. I could not believe it. He had said no to me twelve years previously because I didn't have a graduate degree. Here he had a chance to get us home, and he was not taking it?

Looking back four years later, it is easy to say that God is sovereign. I may have said it at the time, but I wasn't quite sure I meant it or that I truly believed it. I can remember waking up in the middle of the night and going to the living room to cry so I wouldn't wake my husband. I cried and cried, "There is no way out." I could not see a way that my husband could get a job that would pay enough to allow me to stay at home.

And I think that is where God wanted me to be. Fully and completely relying on him. I finally gave up my plan, my way, and my idea.

And a miracle occurred. My brother-in-law called and offered my husband a job. Long story, but believe me, we had not even considered that to be a remote possibility. God worked in the situation and in his heart. He paid for our move to North Carolina. And we came home! Literally. We bought my childhood home. You can still hear the rejoicing of a family confident that God chose this path for them. God received the glory and the praise.

The job my husband has is clearly the one God has chosen for our family at this time. God provides but not always in the way we want or dream. For me, that is usually a good thing. My emotions tend to get in the way–but not of this plan. I know we are where God wants us to be. There have been good times and difficult times over the last four years since we moved to North Carolina. But beyond a shadow of a doubt, God has led us here.

As I settled into my new role as a stay-at-home mother of two, I found myself facing new issues. I had everything I thought I wanted.

My husband was employed. I was at home. Things were tight, but we could pay our bills. So what was wrong? I had this nagging lack of joy.

My circumstances had miraculously changed. I thought that my circumstances were weighing me down. But as the months went by, I realized that the change I desired could only come from God's Holy Spirit working in my life.

God loves me. I know that with my mind, but sometimes it is hard to transfer that knowledge to my feelings. I give thanks for the ways he answers prayers. When everyday feelings get the better of me, I remind myself of all he has done. The longer I walk with God, the more amazed I am that he sent his Son to die for me. That is enough. Or it should be enough. In addition, my life is filled with milestones of how God has provided housing, cars, and jobs far beyond our expectations and dreams.

Yet I still struggle with believing that God will provide the day-to-day cute clothes for my children, shoes (OK, cute shoes), and decorations for our home. And I struggle with being joyful–focusing on God's redeeming love for me in the midst of everyday life. Our budget is limited. So I choose conveniences carefully. I cook seven nights a week. I iron my husband's shirts and slacks. My two-year-old doesn't go to preschool. We don't have cable TV, and we subscribe to a free E-mail service.

As I updated our family room, I ran into a place where I desired to put some greenery. You notice that I say "desired," not "needed." It is a special spot next to the fireplace, in front of the window where I sit every morning to meet with God. I want this special place to be relaxing, comfortable, and inviting. But do I "need" it? I feel like it is similar to my children's clothing issue. My young, growing children "need" clothing. (Especially my six-year-old boy who by January of his kindergarten year had a hole in every single one of his seven pairs of pants. I patched to no avail as he soon had holes in the patches!) But I "want" them to have cute clothes. You know, the matching outfits to have those beautiful family portraits made?

So back to my "desire" to finish my cozy corner of my family room. One day I popped in a small decorative accent store to look around for ideas. And I saw it. Now I am not one of these people who can take a $2 garage sale find, polish and paint it, and make it the knockout centerpiece for the dining room table. I am generally just the opposite. I see something I like. I measure it. I go home. I contemplate. I deliberate. I think. Then I decide to buy it. And I go back to the store, and it is gone!

But when I saw this topiary, I knew it was "it." It stood about three feet high, English ivy surrounding a copper cone. In the middle was a square covered in moss. A rod held all of it secured in a snazzy little planter. I couldn't believe it was exactly what I wanted.

The price: $200. Yikes! I am as frugal as they come. Yet I don't mind paying money for something special: a quality rug, a portrait of my child. But a $200 accessory was way out of the question for me.

Now I did not feel comfortable praying that God would give me a $200 topiary. "God will provide all of your needs." I did not "need" that topiary. But in my view of God, I limited the depth to which God loves and cares for every fiber of my being. Do I allow myself to believe that he truly cherishes me as his child?

I went back to the store. I measured and studied it. I sketched it at home and tried to figure out how to make it. I couldn't find a big brass cone.

Then guess what happened? The accessory store went out of business. I watched the prices go from 25 percent off to 40 percent off. My topiary was still there. I thought maybe at 75 percent I could get it for my birthday. But no. The store quickly closed right after the 40 percent sale. The end?

Not exactly. A couple of months later a friend asked me to go to a local benefit rummage sale. It is a big deal in our town, held at the convention center. I had never been. (I couldn't imagine it being worth the $2 they charged just to get in the doors.) But I went with her for fun—with very low expectations.

We worked our way through the crowd. And there it was! My topiary. I couldn't believe it! It was $25. Brand new! The store had donated their merchandise to this benefit. Passed over by throngs of people who would not spend $25 on a piece of "rummage." God saved it for me.

Every morning as I sit in my special chair to meet with God, I am reminded of his great, overwhelming love for me. God loves me. My big needs and my small heart's desires. He provides me with his Holy Spirit in order to live a joyful, contented life. I have a tangible reminder of the graceful care he gives.

As I dwell on what God has given me–the promise of eternity with him, I can't help but think about what he has rescued me from. It's not something I want to dwell on–eternity without him. But I find it often helps my "joy" quotient. God chose me. He rescued me. I will be with him forever. After I "have suffered a little while"(1 Pet. 5:10–11), he will rescue me and make me strong.

God didn't say that life would be easy. Nor did he promise that we would be prosperous. An easy, prosperous life does not necessarily guarantee joy. In fact, it's encouraging for me to reflect on Paul's journey–being rescued from privilege. Paul had an enviable career path. He had a superb pedigree (Gal. 1:13–14). And he gave it up, threw it away. In exchange? He was beaten, stoned, jailed, scorned . . . and had joy. True joy.

To me joy often seems evasive. You trade one set of challenges in for a completely new set. If you choose to leave the workforce, be prepared for some surprises. Give yourself a year to adjust to life at home. Depending on the age of your children and your financial situation, it may take longer.

Many days during the time that I managed a large staff I longed for an hour to go by without an interruption, crisis, or some need. However, the loneliness and isolation of staying home with a newborn and a two-year old was a huge shock for me. Compound the isolation by a financial situation that didn't allow for preschool outings to McDonalds and even participating in Bible studies where child-care expenses were required.

I could have been easily discouraged. By God's grace I held firm to the commitment my husband and I made. (This was helped by the fact that we had moved a thousand miles away, and I could not readily go back to my old place of employment.) No matter which side of the fence you are sitting on, the grass always looks greener. Making decisions about working outside the home, going part-time, or staying home need to be made with your mind—not your emotions. God will rescue those who love him (Ps. 91:14).

Know why you are choosing what you are choosing. And then give your plan time in order to determine if it is right for you. Be prepared for the unexpected. A change of any type is often harder than you may expect. I've found that God often calls me "to something" rather than "away from something." But the only way I know what he has for my next step is to sit at his feet and seek him. I struggled deeply with my lack of joy in my new situation. I took a deep, hard look at my heart. I could have run. In fact, I sometimes find it is easier to fill my day with to-do lists. It is hard to be Mary in a Martha Stewart world. It is hard to make the time. But the seemingly elusive joy issue is no mystery. God tells us clearly: "Remain in me, and I will remain in you" (John 15:4).

I have some friends that wrote a catchy little tune with these words, so it easily echoes in my head. The tune goes on to paraphrase John 15:5: "Remain in me, and you will bear much fruit." That's it—what I've been looking for! I want the joy that comes as part of the fruit-of-the-Spirit package.

## LESLIE EICHELBERGER

I'm a twenty-nine-year old housewife and expectant mother with our first child, and I have a testimony! My husband and I moved to Mississippi a little over a year and a half ago from Denver, Colorado, because of his job transferring him. While in Denver, he came home one day and said that the Lord put it on his heart to talk to me about our solely living on his income. At the time I worked for a successful interior design firm (in which I have a degree) and was making pretty good money. We talked about it a lot and decided just to pray on it a little more and decided that it would be the right thing to do since the Lord said to do it. Within a month of this new adjustment, our lives changed dramatically. The post office in Hattiesburg contacted my husband and wanted him to report there in three weeks! And the following week I was diagnosed with a fibroid tumor in my uterus that my surgeon scheduled to remove that Thursday, which meant that I would have to leave my job right away! The move and the surgery went well thanks to a lot of praying and help from friends and our church family.

Upon finding an apartment, which happened to be in Petal, we tried to figure out exactly how we could make it on my husband's income, especially after the expensive move and all of the various deposits on rent and utilities. Again the power of prayer proved to be amazing. Within four months of our being here, the Lord blessed my husband with two step increases in his pay where he now makes what we made together in Denver, and we're buying a home.

All that had happened to us up to this point were things we had discussed because my being at home to raise children is important to us both.

Life was going well except for one thing: I still wasn't getting pregnant. My old doctor and my new one here both said that they weren't optimistic because of an infection they found during the surgery. They said that if I had not conceived within six months after the surgery, I needed to look at other options. I didn't want to hear this, and I definitely wasn't planning to seek "other options," so I refused to have any more testing done. I politely but firmly told my doctor that if God wants me to have children, then I will, and if he doesn't, then I won't, and we'll just have to adjust. My faith told me that I was doing the right thing, and Jesus has never let me down! So again we prayed, and then we kind of left it alone and got on with our lives. This happened in March 1999. In September of the same year, I found out that I was pregnant, and the baby and I were and still are very healthy! I'm due to give birth in May!

All Christian women, whether working or not, should try to pattern themselves after the virtuous woman in Proverbs 31. I truly believe that because my husband and I try our best to be obedient to God's Word and structure our family life the way He intended, we have received an abundance of mercy, grace, and blessings that otherwise would not have happened.

## WENDIE REAVES

What an honor to be able to encourage those of you who stay at home with your children and those of you who are diligently working toward that goal. I strongly believe God has a calling for each of us in life. Right now, in my life, he has called me to stay at home with our baby girl.

When I was pregnant with our daughter, Regan, God revealed a job opportunity in another state for my husband. I left my teaching position, and we quickly moved. Several months later our daughter was born. When she was about six months old, we began to notice some developmental problems. Soon it was revealed to us that she was born with a rare neurological disorder. She has several weekly therapy appointments, and we do exercises at home for building strength and gross motor skills. Looking back, I see God's hand in her life all along. We lived in a fairly small town in Arkansas where pediatric therapy might not have been available. Here we are about ten minutes away from Regan's therapist. Also there are numerous other facilities and opportunities here. Being able to stay at home with my daughter has been a gift and a blessing from God.

I'm not going to tell you that everything has been easy. Financially speaking, there were times when I looked at the pile of bills versus the balance in the checkbook and didn't know how the money would stretch, but it always did. And sometimes, on the days we were really desperate, there would be a check in the mailbox. I think one important aspect of our story is that we tithe. I admit, sometimes it is difficult to step out in faith when we are not sure how we'll make ends meet, but God will always honor our gifts. Also, my husband and I have had to give up some hobbies and comforts in order for me to stay home. We have only one vehicle, we rarely eat out, we have virtually zero spending money, and we stick to buying the things we really need. That may sound strange or terrible to some people, but we rarely miss these "things."

Someday, when our daughter looks back on her childhood, the things we did not have won't matter much. But she will know her mom was always there to take care of her, play with her, kiss her, and hug her when she needed it. And, as I write this today, I sit in my home and look at my beautiful girl. She grows and changes so fast, and I don't miss a thing. Yes, I am truly blessed.

## CARA SLUSHER

When I learned that a book was being written about stay-at-home moms, I was excited about the possibility of sharing my own experience with you. I had been a working mom for six years, leaving both of my children in child care from the age of six weeks. Though I was very headstrong about my career, God used a series of events which led me home.

First, I was put in a position that caused me to leave home at least three days a week without seeing my children awake before I left. I was irritable and short of patience with the hectic schedule we kept. Then, one day my three-year-old daughter was rocking her baby doll and was apparently trying to console the crying baby. I thought this action was so sweet and loving, but then I heard Allison say, "Don't cry. Your mom will be here soon." My heart was broken because Allison didn't know how to play "mother." She only knew how to play child-care worker. Finally, and the most important reason, is that God was speaking to me in such a clear and peaceful way to come home that I could no longer resist. Every time I said, "But God," God said, "I'll take care of it."

I submitted my resignation in September 1997. At that time my husband and I stepped out in total faith and submission to God. When I quit, not only was our household income cut in two, but we went from paying $100 a month for excellent insurance to $232 a month for mediocre insurance. However, God saw our need, and in the last three years that mediocre insurance has become great insurance. You see, shortly after I stopped working, our premiums were reduced by $60 a month. Also, the plan has added optical and dental coverage at no extra cost. They have implemented a prescription policy, which allows us to pay a maximum of $15 per prescription. As another benefit, the co-payment was removed this year along with the deductible, and the coverage was increased from a 70/30 payment plan. God is so incredibly good! There is no way my husband and I could have foreseen these events, but through faith in God we received more than we could have imagined.

Yet another example of God's faithfulness was in the area of automobiles. My husband and I each had a car, but both had well over one hundred thousand miles on them. Approximately one year after I began staying at home, the air conditioner went out on my husband's car. The cost to have the repair was greater than the value of the car, and since my husband travels regularly, we swapped cars. I began to pray for a new vehicle at that point because summertime in the South with two children in a non-air-conditioned car is not a fun experience. I told God that he had called me home and that we couldn't afford a new car, so he would have to provide a vehicle.

While traveling, my husband called me with the great news that he had found a car for me. The car had been donated to a nonprofit organization and was now for sale. I was a little skeptical at first because I thought surely it must be a junker. He then explained that the car was a 1990 Chevrolet Celebrity Wagon, which at the time made it only eight years old. The car was in excellent condition with only eighty thousand miles, great tires, and best of all, air-conditioning. I then had to ask the dreaded question about the cost. I almost had to sit down when my husband told me that the car cost only $150! That was the total price! At that moment I thanked God because I knew such a gift could only come from him. That car served us faithfully for the next two years, at which time we were able to afford something else.

I never cease to be amazed at how God has provided for us in our time of need. I know that he is faithful to us because we obeyed him when he called me home. I also know that these examples will not happen to everyone, but I do know that God sees our heart and our needs, and he provides for his children at just the right time.

I know the blessings I have mentioned have been financial, but let's face it: that is an important concern to most women who leave the workforce to stay at home. However, let me tell you the most unmeasurable blessing of all. I am now able to spend time with my children as I never have before in their lives. I greet them at the door every afternoon with a hug, a kiss, and a "How was your day?" Even better, we have summers to play, swim, and participate in Bible school and other activities. I am able to work in their classrooms and have served as homeroom mother for the past three years. Now that my youngest is in kindergarten, I also get to volunteer some time in both of their classrooms. But most of all, and this is the best, both of my children tell me that I am the best mom ever! I can tell you that those words are better and more rewarding than any salary I ever received.

"Trust in the LORD with all your heart and lean not on your own understanding; in all your ways acknowledge him, and he will make your paths straight" (Prov. 3:5–6.)

## EADIE KOLBO

When a woman decides to stay home, I believe it is because her heart longs to be with her children. I also believe that God blesses this. His blessings come in many different ways; some are financial, some are emotional, and some are spiritual.

It's no secret that living on one income these days is a sacrifice. We get paid once a month, and it is very upsetting to be out of money once bills are paid. But without fail, God has provided for us every single month. The provisions became greater when we tithed consistently and from our hearts.

There was a time when we didn't tithe because we had just enough to pay bills, and we thought that if we tithed, some bill wouldn't get paid. We had so little faith. One month I even blurted out to God, "If I pay you, then I'll have to charge the groceries!" God, through his Word, explained to me that the money wasn't ours, but his; he gave it to us. Now we needed to give a small portion back. I felt him telling me to trust him. So we began to tithe . . . and pray! And provisions began to appear right when we needed them. Someone would give us hand-me-down clothes. I began to coupon shop to save us money and discovered how rebates can add up. People who garden shared their beautiful plants with me. Several opportunities "popped up" for my husband to bring home extra income.

The most incredible example of God's providing our finances was just a few months ago. I was paying bills, and we were short $658. I didn't know where we would get the money. Something told me to go back through the checkbook and check for things that hadn't cleared in a year or more. (Always listen to that "little something." It may be God!) Looking closely, I realized that I had recorded a couple of payments twice (paid once, recorded twice). Once I added these amounts together, I sat with my jaw open for a long time. I couldn't believe the amount had added up to exactly $658.91! How great is our God!

When I was in the workplace (before children), my reward was my paycheck. Making money was gratifying. I have four children, and sometimes at the end of the day, I look around and think: *Where is my reward for all my hard work?* God is also faithful to provide in this emotional area. When a teacher or a parent compliments any one of my children for good behavior, I feel so rewarded. I hear "cha-ching!" and realize that I just received my paycheck! All of my daily hard work has manifested itself in the good behavior of my children. However, even in the midst of their misbehavior, God is quick to reassure me that all my efforts are not going unnoticed by him. For example, one day I was in a store with my children. During a bathroom break we agreed to meet at the water fountain outside the bathroom. When I emerged, there were my two boys with wet shirts, wet faces, wet hair. I looked at the floor, and it too was wet. They had been spitting water at each other. I marched them to the manager's office and made them tell the manager what they had done and apologize for not respecting his property. My eyes were filled with tears when I left the office because I felt like my efforts were not paying off. About three minutes later an elderly gentleman came up to me. He said, "I just want you to know that I saw you make those boys apologize back there. You're doing a good job. You don't see many mothers these days willing to do that." That man will never know what that meant to me, but God did, and he knew I needed to hear it. Thank you for my paycheck, mister. "Cha-ching!"

I never knew that being a stay-at-home mom would provide spiritual blessings also, but they have poured forth. There have been countless times (as with all parents), when I've had to make a decision the kids don't like. They cannot see the logic. But being older and wiser (and around the block a few times), I can see what they cannot. God opened my eyes to reveal that the same concept applies with him and me. He said, "Eadie, trust me. I am older and wiser, and I know what's best." It's easy to trust him when I think of it in this manner. There are many analogies like this one that God has allowed me to see, and it comes from being a hands-on parent. The relationship between parents and children can teach us more about our relationship with our heavenly Father and how he loves us and guides us. There are so many similarities between the two. Being a stay-at-home mother has brought me many, many spiritual blessings and will bring me more, I'm sure.

The decision to be a stay-at-home mother is a big one. It will change your life. But more importantly it will change your children's lives. When God calls you to do a job, and for me it is mothering, he will thoroughly equip you. He would not ask you to do something so important and then not provide everything you need to accomplish the task. If God is calling you to stay home with your children, trust him.

## RHONDA KEITH

I do not remember when I started praying that God would provide a way for me to be home with my children. I know that it was before I was pregnant with my first child, Whitney. My mom stayed home with me, my brother, and sister when we were young, and I wanted to be able to do the same for my children. I wanted to give them a firm foundation with lots of love, encouragement, and stability.

When my daughter was eight weeks old, I went back to work. Although I did not make that much money, we did not think we could afford for me to stay at home. We were in a mobile home and were in the process of building our first home. I was miserable leaving her every day. It seemed that as soon as I finished cooking supper and cleaning the dishes, it was time to put Whitney to bed and start getting ready for the next day. It broke my heart that I had so little time to spend with my baby girl. I cried myself to sleep many times and prayed that God would provide a way for me to come home.

He did that and so much more. Six weeks after returning to work, I wrote my resignation letter. I came home with my baby and started keeping another little girl my daughter's age. I was so thankful. God lifted a heavy burden off me.

Three months later my husband, Brad, and his family sold their business. Our income was gone, and we had a new baby and a new house. We prayed that God would open a door for us. While Brad was looking for a good, permanent job, a friend of ours offered him a temporary job with his company. Within a month God provided Brad with a new job, and we never missed a paycheck. God is so awesome!

We had to make sacrifices, of course. Brad's new company was relocating us to Andalusia, Alabama, a nice, small town in the southern part of the state. Leaving our families, friends, and church was hard. Also, we had to sell our new home.

After living in Alabama for nine months, we found that I was pregnant again. We were not planning on that for another year. We wanted to move back home. I prayed that God would either bring us back home or help us feel more at home in Alabama. In the next three months, I experienced a lot of morning sickness. I was more homesick than ever. One night, while I was praying, I felt God reassuring me that he was going to make a way for us to come home. Brad found a job back home making less money, but that was OK with us. After Brad's boss got his resignation letter, he called and offered Brad a position back home. God is so faithful!

We have been home a little over a year now. Soon after we had our second child, Micah, we moved into our second new home (almost identical to the first). God has blessed us more than words can express.

Recently, we have felt God burdening us to get out of debt. We sold our truck and paid off some bills. After we build up our savings, we are going to cut up our credit cards. It has been an adjustment moving back down to one car, but it has been worth it to be more financially free. We plan to purchase our next vehicle with cash in about a year. We have a lot of saving to do.

God has been doing so much in our lives. Making the decision to come home with my children has been the best one Brad and I ever made. I am fulfilling the purpose God has for me and my children. During the ups and downs we have experienced financially, I have never questioned my being at home rather than in the workplace. Brad and I both know where I am needed the most–right here with Whitney and Micah.

## Debbie Kennedy

I vaguely remember a time when, as a nurse, I would work eight to nine hours at a clinic and then rush over to the hospital to catch another shift until midnight. It was an exciting time. I was fresh out of nursing school, and each day was a challenge. (I also recall sleeping late and taking off on weekend trips "just for something to do," but that's another story altogether!) Although I still enjoy nursing and am able to work about eight hours a week, these days my challenges are met on the home front with my husband Mike and our two children: Rushton, four, and Mycah, who is two.

It would be difficult to pinpoint the exact time that God instilled in my heart the desire to stay at home with my children. It was a gradual process that actually began long before they were born. It started when I met my husband and our relationship grew. One of our hopes and dreams became to have a home in which our children would be loved and nurtured and to be present in that home on a constant basis to provide that love.

Because God cultivated this dream so early in our marriage, we were drawn to plan each step of our lives toward that goal. Buying a home, changing jobs, selling our home and building another, changing jobs again, and, most recently, buying a van were all decisions weighed by the question, how will this affect our decision for me to stay at home with our children? We knew that God had already verified that decision and that he would provide a way to accomplish his goal.

If God calls you to stay at home on a daily basis with your children, he will provide a way. After ten years of marriage and two children, he still verifies our decision daily. Sometimes it is in a tangible way. We have always believed in the blessing of tithing, and God has been faithful to provide for us financially. I am not an excellent money manager. There are times when my budget is a mess, or I have made purchases I didn't pray about. But again God shows his faithfulness in tangible ways.

The intangible ways are my favorites! The time my son, who was two and a half, insisted on praying for elephants each night following an outing to the zoo. The joy Mycah exhibits over a bottle of bubbles. Mixed in with breakfast, lunch, and mid-afternoon snack (as well as dishes and diapers from each) are precious moments. Before I paint a picture of blissful days and carefree evenings, however, let me assure you that there are frustrating days and chaotic evenings. Our favorite time of the evening is eight o'clock, as little ones go to bed and my husband and I have a couple hours of peace. But when the morning comes and little voices call from their beds and I get the daily question, "Mom, what are we going to do today?" I am once again thankful to God for being a stay-at-home mom.

God provided for these families, and he can provide for your family. Are you willing to trust him?

**Scripture to Ponder**

"And my God shall supply all your needs according to His riches in glory in Christ Jesus" (Phil. 4:19).

**Action Step**

Make a list of all the different ways God has provided for your family over the years.

CHAPTER 16

# Final Destination

## MARY AND ETHAN

The shortest distance between a problem and a solution
is the distance between your knees and the floor.
The man who kneels to God can stand up to anything.

—Anonymous

## MARY

One hundred years from now where will you be? Well, I am sure of one thing: you won't be worrying about how to pay bills or where the money will come from to send Junior to college. The older I get, the more I realize the brevity of life.

We are told in Hebrews 13:5, "Keep your lives free from the love of money and be content with what you have, because God has said, 'Never will I leave you; never will I forsake you.' So we say with confidence, 'The Lord is my helper; I will not be afraid.'"

One hundred years from now, you and I will be experiencing eternity. I am so glad that more than twenty-five years ago I made the most important investment I could ever make. I gave my life to Jesus Christ.

Before I did this, I was in spiritual darkness. As I shared in my book *My Heart's at Home* (Broadman & Holman, 1999):

I was a good person—probably tried to be too good. I definitely wanted to please other people and thought if I could do enough good works, then maybe I could get to heaven one day. I imagined some sort of massive scale in heaven. Saint Peter would put my good works on one side and my bad works on the other side. I would watch

168

nervously to see which side would tip the scale. How I hoped it would be the good works!

Hoping for eternity. Trying–and yet falling short time and time again. It was so frustrating. I just had a void within me and knew that I could never be good enough to merit eternal life. Yes, I definitely believed that Jesus Christ died on the cross for sins, but I did not believe that he died for MY sins. I thought I had to work my way to heaven. It was as though someone had a wonderful present for me that I was trying to earn. Yet in reality, I could only receive it when I willingly accepted it as a free gift.

I was like someone in a darkened area of Little Rock who refused to turn on the lights after the power had been restored. Why wouldn't I flip the electrical switch? Because I did not understand how the power had been restored. I did not have the faith. And so I continued in darkness.

I am glad that in reality I did not continue living in spiritual darkness. Through friends and Campus Crusade for Christ, the Holy Spirit opened up my eyes to the truth found in Scripture:

"Brothers, my heart's desire and prayer to God for the Israelites is that they may be saved. For I can testify about them that they are zealous for God, but their zeal is not based on knowledge. Since they did not know the righteousness that comes from God and sought to establish their own, they did not submit to God's righteousness. Christ is the end of the law so that there may be righteousness for everyone who believes" (Rom. 10:1–4).

"That if you confess with your mouth, 'Jesus is Lord,' and believe in your heart that God raised him from the dead, you will be saved. For it is with your heart that you believe and are justified, and it is with your mouth that you confess and are saved. As the Scripture says, 'Anyone who trusts in him will never be put to shame'" (Rom. 10:9–11).

I had finally found the answer. I realized that I could never, *never*, never be good enough to merit eternal life, and I recognized that only a perfect God could pay for the sin against a holy Creator. The lights went on in my heart. I admitted that I was a sinner who could not earn her way to heaven, and I said a prayer accepting Jesus Christ as my personal Lord and Savior. At that point I had new life and an eternal destination (1 Pet. 1:23). Just as the light was restored to a dark downtown area, so too did light flood my life. The void in me was gone forever.

I remember asking myself, "Why would the God of the universe become man and willingly allow himself to die on a cross? Why wouldn't he have chosen another way for salvation—an easier, less painful way?"

We cannot understand the mind of God. We cannot comprehend his unmatchable splendor and holiness. Isaiah 55:8-9 tells us, "For my thoughts are not your thoughts, neither are your ways my ways," declares the Lord. "As the heavens are higher than the earth, so are my ways higher than your ways and my thoughts than your thoughts." Even Moses was told in Exodus 33:20, "You cannot see my face, for no one may see me and live."

Holiness. There are few examples of holiness today. No wonder it is hard for many to believe by faith that Jesus Christ died on the cross for their sins. Only the death of the perfect God-man could pay the penalty of sin. And to think that he willingly died on a cross for Adam's sin, for Eve's sin, for yours, and mine.

We are told in Romans 10:4, "Christ is the end of the law so that there may be righteousness for everyone who believes."

Romans 6:23 explains that "the wages of sin is death." Even when I tried to lead a sinless life, I just could not do it. That's why I was so thrilled when I learned that by putting my trust in a perfect Savior, Jesus Christ, then my sins were forgiven forever.

I am so glad that I know the address of my eternal home; it's heaven. I am certain of this not because of any good work that I have done but entirely because of the finished work that Jesus Christ did on the cross for me. I could not save myself, but I could humble myself, recognizing that I would never be good enough for heaven, and accept the free gift of salvation. And that is exactly what I did!

Once you have made the most important decision of your life—where you will spend eternity—then it's important to follow God's blueprints for life which are found in Scripture. The advice in God's Word is sound and practical. After all, the Bible is actually our instruction manual from our Maker!

The following is an excerpt from an E-mail that I received. The author was not given.

> God won't ask what kind of fancy car you drove. He will ask how many people you took to church who didn't have transportation.
>
> God won't ask the square footage of your house. He will ask how many people you helped who didn't have a house.
>
> God won't ask how many fancy clothes you had in your closet. He will ask how many of them you gave away.
>
> God won't ask how many material possessions you had. He will ask whether those material possessions dictated your life.

Mom, I think you and I need constantly to be on our knees asking God to direct our steps. Maybe you are thinking, *I want to focus more on God's will for my family than I do the financial concerns of my family.* Give this desire to God. Ask him to help this desire become a reality.

Another favorite E-mail that I recently received contains a lot of wisdom. It says, "The shortest distance between a problem and a solution is the distance between your knees and the floor. The man who kneels to God can stand up to anything."

Take your cares to Jesus. He can handle them and give you the rest that you long for.

## ETHAN

This could very well be the most important chapter in this book because you will be challenged with the most important question: if you were to die today, do you know where you would spend eternity?

Let me briefly share with you about my spiritual journey. In the fall of 1975, Chip Scivicque, Greg Kelly, and Jim Craft, who were on staff with Campus Crusade for Christ, spoke at my fraternity house on the campus of the University of Mississippi. Several days after this meeting I personally came to an understanding of what it means to know Jesus Christ as my personal Savior. Even though I was a good moral person and faithfully attended church every week, I had never seriously considered what it meant to be a Christian until that day. I had always believed that if you were "good" surely you were a Christian. Or another way to put it, if your good works outweighed your bad ones, you would go to heaven. (Depending 100 percent on your good works no more makes you a Christian than walking into a garage makes you a car!)

Chip shared with me a small yellow booklet called the *Four Spiritual Laws* written by Bill Bright. The first law states that "God loves you and has a wonderful plan for your life." The second law is, "Man is sinful and separated from God: therefore he cannot know and experience God's love and plan for his life." The Bible says that we are all sinners and separated from God (Rom. 3:23) and that "the wages of sin is death" (Rom. 6:23). Law three is, "Jesus Christ is God's only provision for man's sin. Through Him you can know and experience God's love and plan for your life." In other words, Jesus is the *only way* to God. "I am the way, and the truth, and the life; no one comes to the Father, but through Me" (John 14:6 NASB). However, it is not enough just to know these three laws. Law four states, "We must individually receive Jesus Christ as Savior and Lord; then we can know and experience God's love and plan for our lives." "For by grace you have been saved through faith; and that not of yourselves, it is the gift of God; not as a result of works, that no one should boast" (Eph. 2:8–9 NASB).

I bowed my head, confessed my sins, asked for forgiveness, surrendered my life, and invited Jesus Christ to come into my heart. I simply said a prayer like this: "Lord Jesus, I need you. Thank you for dying on the cross for my sins. I open the door of my life and receive you as my Savior and Lord. Thank you for forgiving my sins and giving me eternal life. Take control of my life and make me the kind of person you want me to be. Amen."

I didn't hear any angels singing or firecrackers exploding after I prayed that prayer, but I knew that I had established a personal relationship with Jesus Christ. That's right. It's a relationship with Jesus Christ, not a religion with a long list of dos and don'ts.

If the prayer that I prayed expresses the desire of your heart and you want to establish a personal relationship with Jesus Christ, I would like to encourage you to pray it right now and invite Jesus into your life! Tell a trusted Christian friend, plug in with a local church, and seek guidance from Christians who can help you grow in your new faith. Also, please write and let me know of your decision. My address is at the back of this book. I have some free material that will help you to grow as a Christian that I would love to send you.

**Scriptures to Ponder**

"Therefore, there is now no condemnation for those who are in Christ Jesus, because through Christ Jesus the law of the Spirit of life set me free from the law of sin and death" (Rom. 8:1–2).

"For God so loved the world that he gave his one and only Son, that whoever believes in him shall not perish but have eternal life" (John 3:16).

**Action Step**

Write down on paper why you know you will spend eternity with God. (If you cannot do this, talk with a Christian friend or Christian pastor about this.)

CHAPTER 17

# Common Questions and Answers

ETHAN AND MARY

If any of you lacks wisdom, he should ask God, who gives
generously to all without finding fault, and it will be given to him.

–James 1:5

**Q: Is it possible for a family to live on one income?**

A: [Ethan] Naturally the more income a family has coming in, the easier the goal will be to accomplish. However, I know of some families earning $85,000 per year who could not "imagine" having to scale back, while I know of other families earning less than $20,000 and living on one income. So, to answer your question, yes, it is possible, but in most cases it comes down to priorities. How willing are you (and the family) to give up a few things in order for mom to remain at home?

**Q: Is it wrong for a mom to work outside the home?**

A: [Ethan] Let me approach it this way. I believe that most people would agree that it is better if mom could be home with the kids, especially during the early years of life. The biblical role is for the man to be the provider for the family and the woman to be the nurturer. It's hard to nurture a child while you are at work and the child is in child care. My biblical conviction is that we should be doing everything possible to allow moms to remain at home with the kids.

A: [Mary] I agree totally with what Ethan said. But I'd like to add that I can find nowhere in Scripture where it says that it is a sin for a mom to work outside of the home. However, I know firsthand how hard it is to juggle home and work responsibilities–especially with young children. I believe that it is best for mom to be at home when the children are at home. They grow up so quickly, and you can never recapture their childhoods.

**Q: Do you think it is acceptable for a mom to work while the children are in school?**

A: [Ethan] There are definite seasons in a family's life. My desire would be for a mom to be at home 100 percent of the time during the preschool years of a child's life. Then, if financially necessary, maybe mom could work part-time during school hours. This way, mom is still at home when the children need her most.

A: [Mary] I agree.

**Q: Why are most books like this written to women, when in reality, it's the man who needs to begin taking more responsibility for his family?**

A: [Ethan] That is a great question, and I agree that men do need to take more responsibility for the direction of their family. This book was not written to give moms a guilt trip and let dads off the hook! Be assured that every dad will stand before the Lord and give an accounting of how he led his family. Dads don't have the freedom to be completely absent from home at all times. If a dad is committed to his family, even though he has a full-time job, he will be committed to spend time with his family during the evenings and weekends. For more information about dads, be sure you read chapter 13.

**Q: How do I encourage my husband to help more around the home?**

A: [Ethan] Being the financial provider for the family does not exempt your spouse from his roles as husband and dad. As a servant-leader, he needs to help you willingly around the house and also spend time with the children. I suggest that you and your husband sit down and examine your priorities together. Agree on some specific ways that your husband can help you. Also, I see nothing wrong with making a list and posting it on the refrigerator.

A: [Mary] I agree totally with what Ethan said. Also, I have found that sometimes husbands are willing to help but are unaware of a need to help. Cleaning the kitchen to a husband may mean putting the dishes into the sink. My husband, Jim, is a wonderful helpmate. Over the years I have learned that he cannot read my mind. Yet, when I ask Jim to help me in a specific way, he is always willing to pitch in and do whatever is needed.

**Q: What should I do if I desire to stay at home, but my husband is not open to that option?**

A: [Ethan] I would *not* encourage you to spend hours debating the issue with your husband. The best thing you can do is to begin to spend time on your knees asking God to change his heart in this area. If God can change the heart of a king, surely he can change the heart of your husband.

In addition to prayer, you might consider developing a MAP (budget) to present to your husband to show him how it is financially possible for you to remain at home. I believe that most men would love for their wives to have the opportunity to stay at home; however, the financial pressure is just too great. Therefore, if you can convince your husband that you are willing to cut back and sacrifice in order to stay at home with the kids, he just might have a change of heart. Don't forget that God is a big God!

**Q: Is there a way for me really to know what God desires for me as a wife and mother?**

A: [Mary] I think you need to make prayer and time in God's Word top priority. We are told in Psalm 119:105, "Your word is a lamp to my feet and a light for my path." And Proverbs 3:6 promises us, "In all your ways acknowledge him, and he will make your paths straight."

It may sound trite, but I believe that God will open and close his doors for you and me as we follow his Word and are called according to his purpose.

**Q: Do you think it would be acceptable to cut back on our giving (less than 10 percent), in order for me to remain at home?**

A: [Ethan] I am convinced that a family giving 10 percent or more and living on 90 percent or less has a better chance to make it financially than a family that gives 1 percent and keeps 99 percent. Don't short-circuit the potential for God's provision and financial blessings in your life! Nowhere in the Bible does God give a list of reasons where we can opt out of supporting his kingdom. Take God at his Word; he will provide.

**Q: I am really struggling with this issue of giving. What Bible verses could you recommend that I read that might help?**

A: [Ethan] Let me encourage you to read and pray over the great verses on giving: Proverbs 3:9–10; 11:24–26; Haggai 1:3–7; Malachi 3:8–10; Mark 12:41–44; Luke 6:38; 2 Corinthians 8:1–3; 9:1–10.

**Q: Do you have any suggestions for a working single mom?**

A: [Ethan] My heart goes out to you. You are in a position where working (unless you receive a miracle) is your only option. Just be faithful to do your best every day and ask God to help you one day at a time. As I shared earlier, my dad died when I was seven years old, and my mom began teaching school once again. Now as an adult, I know that life was hard for my mom, but I never heard her complain! Just because you have to work as a single parent, it does not mean that you cannot have a great family. Maybe they won't appreciate all you do for them now, but I can assure you, when they grow older, you will become their hero.

A: [Mary] You may want to get a copy of my book *My Heart's at Home*. I believe that it will not only encourage you but also give you some practical tips for juggling home and work responsibilities.

**Q: Why do some moms feel like a failure because they are not working in the marketplace?**

A: [Ethan] Our culture places a high value on careers and little or no value on the importance of raising children! In many families children are more of a nuisance than a blessing. This is not God's perspective on children. God says that children are a blessing from him and we are to treasure them (Ps. 127:1–5).

**Q. I quit work once to stay at home with the children. My husband and I both wanted me to be at home. But we found that we were just financially unable to do this, and I went back to work. Where did we go wrong?**

A: [Mary] I quit work briefly after our oldest son was born. Our mistake was poor planning. We liked the idea of my staying home, but we didn't have a financial plan for making this desire a reality. About a month before I quit work, my husband became self-employed. In retrospect, it is so easy to see what a bad idea it was for both of us to give up dependable salaries simultaneously. And to top it off, our oldest son was born two months prematurely. So, add medical bills to it all, and it is easy to see why this did not work.

And we were not alone. I have known many moms who have quit work to return to work after a matter of months.

I want to encourage you not to give up. Follow Ethan's practical, biblical advice in this book. You might not be able to quit work entirely tomorrow, but with a plan you know where you are heading. And with God's help, your desires will become reality.

**Q. What do I do with my regrets? I've missed some valuable years with my child that I can't take back.**

A: [Mary] Cling to the fact that God is sovereign over all, and if we will let him, he will work everything out for good—in his time, in his way. Romans 8:28 tells us, "And we know that in all things God works for the good of those who love him, who have been called according to his purpose." If we truly love God and are committed to him, he will transform even our mistakes into something that brings him glory. I like to think that he has allowed many of my mistakes to give birth to this book. And hopefully, it will help you and many other moms!

**Q: We are deep in debt and have no hope. Some of our friends have filed for bankruptcy to relieve the stress. I think**

**I could stay at home if we could wipe the financial slate clean. What do you think?**

A: [Ethan] Two wrongs never make a right. First, as long as you have the Lord, you will always have hope. You need to "yoke" up with Jesus, not your attorney. Jesus said, "Come to Me, all who are weary and heavy-laden, and I will give you rest. Take My yoke upon you and learn from Me, for I am gentle and humble in heart; and YOU WILL FIND REST FOR YOUR SOULS. For My yoke is easy and My load is light" (Matt. 11:28–30 NASB). Find some time, pull out your Bible, and sit there and simply read and meditate on this passage. Turn your burdens over to Jesus. Let him minister to you.

Second, I would not encourage you to file for bankruptcy. If you bought the items and spent the money, you are responsible to repay it. "The wicked borrows and does not pay back" (Ps. 37:21 NASB).

**Q: I have tried many different budgets before, but none seem to work for me. Any suggestions?**

A: [Ethan] You are either using the wrong budget and/or you are not disciplined to follow your plan. Give the MAP system a try. It's simple and easy to use, but it is not a miracle system; it still requires discipline. (See address at back of book to order a year supply of MAPs.)

**Q: Would you summarize what I should do to leave the workplace and move to the home place?**

A: [Ethan] Chapters 6, 7, and 8 are your how-to chapters, but you will also find a great summary list in chapter 11.

CHAPTER 18

# Financial Facts

ETHAN

The wise man saves for the future,
but the foolish man spends whatever he gets.
—Proverbs 21:20 TLB

One of the best ways for families to prepare for Mom to be able to stay at home is to plan ahead. If you presently do not have children, I recommend that you begin to save a portion of your income each month, especially if both you and your husband are working. Just look at the following chart and see how much you can accumulate over a few years! Your savings can play a major part in allowing you to remain at home full-time once you have children! If you sacrifice early in life, you will be able to accomplish your goals later in life. It takes only a little money, saved over a few years, to equal a lot!

You will find charts for investing $100, $250, and $500 per month with returns as low as 4 percent and as high as 12 percent.

I can already see your reaction now. How could I ever invest $500 per month. Well, if you already have children, it's probably impossible. But if you are married, with no children and both husband and wife are working, it just might be possible to save $500 per month if you make it a goal and operate on a budget! I can guarantee you one thing—if you never make it a goal, it will never happen.

# IF YOU INVEST $100 PER MONTH

## RETURN ON INVESTMENT

|       | 4%       | 6%       | 8%       | 10%      | 12%      |
|-------|----------|----------|----------|----------|----------|
| **Years** |      |          |          |          |          |
| 1     | $1,222   | $1,233   | $1,244   | $1,256   | $1,268   |
| 3     | 3,816    | 3,933    | 4,053    | 4,178    | 4,307    |
| 5     | 6,629    | 6,977    | 7,347    | 7,743    | 8,166    |
| 7     | 9,675    | 10,407   | 11,211   | 12,095   | 13,067   |
| 9     | 12,974   | 14,273   | 15,743   | 17,405   | 19,289   |

# IF YOU INVEST $250 PER MONTH

## RETURN ON INVESTMENT

|       | 4%       | 6%       | 8%       | 10%      | 12%      |
|-------|----------|----------|----------|----------|----------|
| **Years** |      |          |          |          |          |
| 1     | $3,055   | $3,083   | $3,112   | $3,141   | $3,170   |
| 3     | 9,545    | 9,834    | 10,133   | 10,445   | 10,769   |
| 5     | 16,574   | 17,442   | 18,369   | 19,359   | 20,417   |
| 7     | 24,188   | 26,018   | 28,028   | 30,237   | 32,668   |
| 9     | 32,435   | 35,605   | 39,357   | 43,513   | 48,233   |

# IF YOU INVEST $500 PER MONTH

## RETURN ON INVESTMENT

|       | 4%       | 6%       | 8%       | 10%      | 12%      |
|-------|----------|----------|----------|----------|----------|
| **Years** |      |          |          |          |          |
| 1     | $6,111   | $6,167   | $6,224   | $6,282   | $6,341   |
| 3     | 19,090   | 19,668   | 20,267   | 20,890   | 21,538   |
| 5     | 33,149   | 34,885   | 36,738   | 38,718   | 40,834   |
| 7     | 48,377   | 52,036   | 56,056   | 60,475   | 65,336   |
| 9     | 64,870   | 71,370   | 78,715   | 87,026   | 96,446   |

Just think how financially helpful it would be if you could save for three or five years before you have children. Now I am not recommending that anyone postpone having children just so they can build up an investment account, but if you presently do not have children, now is a great time to save for your future goals!

In addition to saving before you have children, consider making all your financial decisions on one income. For example, if you are married and both of you are working, when you apply for a mortgage, qualify on only the husband's income. These types of financial decisions will help give you the freedom in the future for Mom to stop working if she desires to.

**Scripture to Ponder**

"In the house of the wise are stores of choice food and oil, but a foolish man devours all he has" (Prov. 21:20).

**Action Step**

Determine how much you can begin to save each month.

## CHAPTER 19

# Our Prayer for You

## ETHAN AND MARY

I lift up my eyes to the hills–where does my help come from?
My help comes from the LORD, the Maker of heaven and earth.

–Psalm 121:1–2

Lord, this is my [Ethan's] prayer for all the moms and dads reading this book.

When they are weak, give them strength.
When they are tired, give them rest.
When they are in financial need, provide for them.
When they are discouraged, lift them up.
When they need answers, give them wisdom.
When they are confused, give them direction.
When they are anxious, give them peace.
When they are lonely, show them your love.
And finally,
When they are fearful, give them faith. Amen

*You can do it, Mom.* Believe in yourself, but most of all believe in a great God. My final challenge and prayer is for you to remember what Gabriel told the mother of Jesus: "For nothing will be impossible with God" (Luke 1:37 NASB). Just like Mary, let me encourage you to treasure these words in your heart as you reach toward your destination and truly find, "There's No Place like Home." And Mom, once you get home, enjoy every minute of it–as I know you will! It has been an absolute joy for me (and Mary) to write this book for you. If I don't see you before, I will see you in heaven. Press on my friend!

🐚 Mom, first, remember that God is faithful! Put your trust in him. The older I (Mary) get, the more I realize that my Lord is the Master Craftsman whose specialty is turning useless coal into priceless gems.

Second, be united with your husband (if you are married) and support his leadership. Pray diligently and follow the steps Ethan described in this book to turn your conviction of being home into a reality.

Third, prayerfully bring your desires to the Lord and ask him to make your path home straight. Find encouragement in Proverbs 16:9, "In his heart a man plans his course, but the LORD determines his steps."

And finally, when you get home, help other moms. I love what David Williams said in his book *Life Lessons and Other Observations*: "There is an old proverb that states, 'Once you take the elevator up, don't forget to send it back down.'"[1]

I'd like to end our journey together with a story that a dear friend shared about her parents. Having lived through the Great Depression, they were terrified about the possibility of a Y2K disaster, and they prepared for the worst. They placed a fairly large sum of money in a glass jar and buried it in their back yard. After many months had passed, my friend's elderly father decided to check on his security for disaster. As he twisted the top off of the dirt-covered jar, he was shocked to find that the money had deteriorated. Rain had apparently seeped into the jar and destroyed it.

Mom, don't bury your dream to be home. And remember the words of 1 Thessalonians 5:24, "The one who calls you is faithful and he will do it."

Ethan and I will be praying for you. After all, there really is no place like home!

# Endnotes

**Introduction**

1. Women's Bureau, U.S. Dept. of Labor, *The World Almanac and Book of Facts,* 1997, 172.

2. Ibid.

3. Ibid.

4. U.S. Dept. of Labor, *1998 Information Please Almanac,* 131.

**Chapter 1**

1. "Better Families," Vol. 19, No. 10, October 1995.

2. Ethan Pope, *How to Be a Smart Money Manager* (Nashville: Thomas Nelson, 1995), 135.

3. *Parade* magazine, April 18, 1999, 4–5.

4. Pope, *How to Be a Smart Money Manager,* 25–26.

**Chapter 2**

1. *The Statistical Handbook of the American Family,* 1999.

2. Paul Harvey, *Conservative Chronicle,* September 22, 1993, 22.

3. *Focus on the Family* magazine, May 1998.

**Chapter 3**

1. *The Wall Street Journal Almanac,* 1998, 408.

2. Ibid., 411.

3. Ann Landers, *Hattiesburg American,* September 6, 1999, 5B.

**Chapter 5**

1. Jerry Bridges, *The Joy of Fearing God* (Colorado Springs, Colo.: Waterbrook Press, 1997). Used by permission.

**Chapter 9**

1. *Arkansas Democrat-Gazette,* August 28, 1999, 13A.

2. Ibid., August 23, 1999, 1D.

3. *Christian Financial Concepts,* December 10, 1999.

## Chapter 12

1. *Leadership,* Summer 1999, 73.
2. *USA Today,* December 31, 1999, 3B.
3. *Arkansas Democrat-Gazette,* November 8, 1999, 1D.
4. *FamiilyLife Parenting Conference Manual,* 1993, 181–96.
5. Barbara Curtis, *Small Beginnings: First Steps to Prepare Your Child for Lifelong Learning* (Nashville: Broadman & Holman Publishers, 1997), 37.
6. *USA Today,* November 8, 1999, 1A.
7. John R. Starr, "A Modern Paradox," *Arkansas Democrat-Gazette,* November 7, 1999, 5J.

## Chapter 13

1. Used with permission from author.

## Chapter 14

1. *Meetings & Conventions,* September 1999, 101–103.
2. Bernard B. Kanoroff, *Small Time Operator* (Willis, Calif.: Bell Springs Publishing, 1998), 13.
3. J. I. Packer, Merrill C. Tenney, and William White Jr.; *The Bible Almanac* (Nashville: Thomas Nelson, 1980), 479.
4. From *Chicken Soup for the Soul: 101 Stories to Open the Heart and Rekindle the Spirit.* This quote was written and compiled by Jack Canfield and Mark V. Hansen, *Communications Briefings* 17: 2.

## Chapter 19

1. David Williams, *Life Lessons and Other Observations* (Gadsden, Ala.: B.A.N.C. Publishing, 1999).

## Share Your Story

Send your letter to the address below and share your story of how God has provided for your family and allowed you to be at home full time.

## For information on:

- Inviting Ethan Pope to speak at your church or other group
- Receiving a catalog of information from Foundations For Living
- Ordering a one-year supply of full-size (8 1/2 x 11) MAP forms
- Ordering the MAP instruction tape: More Fun Less Fights
- Scheduling conferences on this or other topics
- Receiving Foundations For Living publications
- Ordering *How to Be a Smart Money Manager*

## Write to:

Ethan Pope
Foundations For Living Ministry
P.O. Box 15356
Hattiesburg, MS 39404

## Visit Our Web Site:

www.foundationsforliving.org

## For information on:

Inviting Mary Larmoyeux to speak at your church or other group

## Contact Mary at:

www.jlarmoyeux@aristotle.net